BEAUTIFUL CREATURES

THE OFFICIAL ILLUSTRATED MOVIE COMPANION

BY

MARK COTTA VAZ

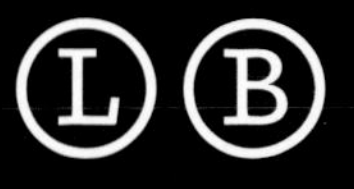

LITTLE, BROWN AND COMPANY

NEW YORK • BOSTON

Little, Brown and Company

Hachette Book Group
237 Park Avenue, New York, NY 10017
Visit our website at www.lb-teens.com

Little, Brown and Company is a division of
Hachette Book Group, Inc.
The Little, Brown name and logo are trademarks of
Hachette Book Group, Inc.

First Edition: January 2013

Book design by Erin McMahon
All photographs by John Bramley unless otherwise credited

Library of Congress Control Number: 2012947605

ISBN 978-0-316-24519-7

10 9 8 7 6 5 4 3 2 1
WOR
Printed in the United States of America

To Kami Garcia, Margaret Stohl, Richard LaGravenese, and the cast and crew of *Beautiful Creatures*. And to the memory of Ralph McQuarrie, visionary artist and mythmaker.

—MCV

The following talented people graciously shared their perspectives on the creative journey of *Beautiful Creatures*:

AUTHORS

Kami Garcia

Margaret Stohl

DIRECTOR, SCREENWRITER

Richard LaGravenese

PRODUCERS

Erwin Stoff

Andrew Kosove

Broderick Johnson

Molly Smith

ART DEPARTMENT

Richard Sherman,
production designer

Lorin Flemming,
art director

Troy Sizemore,
supervising art director

ACTORS

Viola Davis, *Amma*

Zoey Deutch, *Emily Asher*

Alden Ehrenreich,
Ethan Wate

Alice Englert,
Lena Duchannes

Jeremy Irons,
Macon Ravenwood

Emma Thompson,
Mrs. Lincoln

COSTUME, HAIR, & MAKEUP

Jeffrey Kurland,
costume designer

Terry Baliel,
hair department head

Fionagh Cush,
makeup department head

EFFECTS

Joe Harkins,
visual effects supervisor

Matt Kutcher,
special effects supervisor

PROPS

Brook Yeaton,
prop master

STUNTS

Chuck Picerni Jr.,
stunt coordinator

EDITORIAL

David Moritz,
film editor

TABLE OF CONTENTS

CHAPTER 1

Casting a Spell

“Gatlin wasn't like the small towns you saw in the movies, unless it was a movie from about fifty years ago. We were too far from Charleston to have a Starbucks or a McDonald's.... The library still had a card catalog, the high school still had chalkboards, and our community pool was Lake Moultrie, warm brown water and all. You could see a movie at the Cineplex about the same time it came out on DVD, but you had to hitch a ride over to Summerville, by the community college. The shops were on Main, the good houses were on River, and everyone else lived south of Route 9, where the pavement disintegrated into chunky concrete stubble....”

—**Ethan Lawson Wate**, reflecting on his town in *Beautiful Creatures*, the novel[1]

"WE WANTED TO CREATE OUR OWN MAGICAL UNIVERSE."

It started with phrases that appeared like half-remembered fragments from an ancient spell, the first manifestations of a magical tale conjured by two women in Los Angeles. Both were well read, well educated, married with children, and they sealed a creative pact with the determination to defeat the doubts of one strong-willed daughter.

Margaret "Margie" Stohl had been creating fantasy universes for the videogame market, and Kami Garcia was an elementary school teacher and high school English tutor whose students included two of Stohl's daughters. Neither imagined the strange turn their lives would take that day in September 2005 when they had lunch at El Cholo, a Mexican restaurant in Los Angeles. Stohl wanted to write a book and had also been urging Garcia to write about her family's Southern roots. During lunch, a story idea was born as they began scribbling notes on the restaurant's paper napkins. "We wanted to create our own magical universe, and we worked out this wild family tree and this Southern town," Stohl recalled. "When I went home, I said to my daughters, 'Mrs. Garcia'—because that's what they call her—'and I are going to write a book.' And they just laughed at me. And Emma, my oldest daughter, said, 'Mom, you may *think* you'll write a book, but in two days you'll be doing something else, because you never finish anything.' Which was basically true; she was right to laugh. But I was so annoyed at her. I said, 'Oh, it's *on*!' So, basically, it was a bet."

Garcia and Stohl were already a formidable team. Stohl, who first knew Garcia as her daughter's third-grade teacher, learned early on that they shared a love of books, and a friendship was born. "She had an education degree, with a focus on what made kids read, and we're both from storytelling families," Stohl explained. "There's also a lot of the small town in both of us. So we bonded. Sometimes it felt like we were the only two people in LA who still read books. We built classroom libraries together and started trading books back and forth. Both of us liked fantasy books, so Kami started a fantasy book club at my house with my kids and their

Authors Kami Garcia and Margaret Stohl on set with dialect coach Rick Lipton.

friends. It started when they were little, with Tolkien and *Harry Potter*. As young adult literature evolved, we read *Twilight* with them. My daughters are really smart and opinionated, with strong personalities, and they're also fencers. And they were indignant [about] a few points they said kept coming up [as they read young adult literature]. They said, 'Why does the girl always have to fall in love and never be powerful and have to follow the boy around? Why can't the girl be powerful?' When we started writing our book, the kids said, 'Don't be generic, don't have vampires, let the girl be powerful and magical.'"

After brainstorming together to create the key elements of the story, Garcia and Stohl began their first draft. "I'm a word person; certain words interest me and can form an idea. I was haunted by the words *sixteen moons*," said Stohl. "I thought, *What would happen in a book called* Sixteen Moons? And there was this weird smell of lemons and rosemary. So at the beginning I sat down and wrote: *There were sixteen moons, lemons and rosemary*. A weird dream just came out when I started writing. I called up Kami and said, 'Are we really going to do this?' And I sent her a chunk of pages. From there we cobbled together the magical universe."

Garcia's family tree includes

Photo courtesy Richard LaGravenese

The director took a research trip and photographed Southern towns such as McClellanville, South Carolina, for inspiration.

Confederate General Jubal Early, a scourge of Union forces, who was bested by General Philip Sheridan in the Shenandoah Valley Campaign. (Sheridan and his 45,000 men were ordered by General Ulysses Grant to follow Early "to the death" and leave the valley a wasteland.[2]) She grew up in Washington, DC, but her grandmother and great-grandmother, who hailed from a small town in North Carolina, lived with her family from the time she was twelve, and Garcia went back often with them to visit.

"It was like having the South in your house," Garcia recalled. "My friends always wondered why our vegetables tasted so good—I thought *everybody* put bacon grease in their vegetables. My great-grandmother baked everything from scratch and would no more have bought a pie from a store than run around the neighborhood in her britches. I called my great-grandma Nanny, and she was one of those hardworking Southern women who had lost a husband quite young and had to be a seamstress and a laundress and do whatever she could to take care of her kids. She always wore a dress, never pants, and had an apron over it with pockets. That [apron] was like a Mary Poppins bag—if you needed Kleenex, scissors, a ruler, she'd have it in one of those pockets. She made a lot of my clothes, like my dresses for special occasions. She was really beautiful for her age, and I asked her once why she didn't date. She got so offended. 'I'm *married*,' she said, 'and I'm going to see my husband in heaven. I am not going to tell him I was dating. He's probably listening right now, so we should stop talking about this.'"

Although Stohl grew up in Los

> " Kami and I agreed that the South is the place where magic could still exist in the United States, narratively speaking. You believe anything can happen. The buildings are haunted by so much history. "
>
> —**Margaret Stohl**, author

Angeles, she shared with Garcia an affinity for small-town life from summer days spent with her grandmother in Utah. Around 1995, she began designing fantasy worlds for the early video-game industry. "These were some of the first moving pictures, where you could see a video-game graphic image," Stohl recalled. But she remained a "book person" who studied English literature at Amherst College and was "obsessed" with the great Southern writer Eudora Welty, as well as the Mississippi delta.

"What we were interested in for our first book was mood, and that story was so much about mood. It allowed us to shade our town a certain way. That was the kind of magic we were conjuring up, the idea of 'coming out' as a magical person in this small town."

" People in the South don't balk if you say you've seen a ghost—they compare stories to see if their ghost was scarier than yours. I saw my grandfather's ghost when I was nine, right after he died. I was standing in front of a mirror and I saw him standing behind me. When I turned around, he was gone. It wasn't scary. He was smiling and he looked happy, the way he always did when he was alive. "

—**Kami Garcia**, author

That magical person is Lena Duchannes, a newcomer to Gatlin, the story's fictional South Carolina town. She's an instant outsider because she has come to live with her uncle, Macon Ravenwood, a mysterious recluse and object of idle gossip who lives in Ravenwood Manor, a crumbling old plantation house that survived Sherman's slash-and-burn campaign. But Ethan Wate, a popular sixteen-year-old, is drawn to Lena. He even dreams of her before they meet. As they become close, Ethan learns that Lena is a "Caster"—otherwise known as a witch. In the film, December 21 is the date of her impending sixteenth birthday, when she will experience her Claiming, a supernatural coming-of-age during which she

Alice Englert as Lena Duchannes.

will ever after be ruled by the forces of either good or evil (the "Light" or the "Dark")—and she is powerless to affect the outcome.

> "There's sort of a new genre of film now that mixes romance and is grounded in real-life situations, but also has a touch of fantasy that elevates the material."
>
> —**Broderick Johnson**, producer

The tale went from a project vetted by their families and a tight circle of Garcia's students to the prize at a publishing-house auction. "Yeah, it definitely took on a life of its own," marveled Kami Garcia. "We were really writing to win a bet with my teen students and Margie's daughters, who were also my students. The payoff was, we finished and they liked it. We thought we'd make a website for it and get other kids to read it, but we had no idea this was going to be a book. We didn't think about agents and publishers. Then a friend of Margie's read it and gave it to an agent without telling us. Suddenly, an agent called, and it changed the game. It went from being a story living in our computer to the idea of being a book. Even then it was a series of ridiculous magical events that at every juncture seemed too good to be true."

Little, Brown and Company—home to Stephenie Meyer's Twilight Saga series—won the bid and published *Beautiful Creatures* in December 2009. The debut novel was a critically acclaimed bestseller, and the authors continued their saga with *Beautiful Darkness* (2010), *Beautiful Chaos* (2011), and *Beautiful Redemption* (2012). It was important,

The Ravenwood Manor exterior.

The Beautiful Creatures novels: **Beautiful Creatures, Beautiful Darkness, Beautiful Chaos,** ***and*** **Beautiful Redemption.**

and fortuitous, that Julie Scheina, their editor at Little, Brown, was from the South. "Having someone Southern was a really big deal, but it all felt like luck, and the movie was the culmination of that," commented Garcia, referring to the next auction—this time for movie rights. The writing project's charmed life took another astounding turn when Alcon Entertainment and Warner Bros. took *Beautiful Creatures* into production in 2012, with a theatrical release in February 2013.

"We got a call that Richard LaGravenese wanted to read the book, and I was immediately familiar with him from *The Fisher King* and *The Bridges of Madison County* [for which LaGravenese wrote the screenplays, with Terry Gilliam and Clint Eastwood, respectively, directing those pictures]," Garcia said. "Then we found out he wanted to be attached and take it to the studios. We felt lucky to have gotten to that step—at least *he* liked it! But even when it was optioned, Margie would say, 'It'll never get made.'"

Molly Smith, a creative producer with a first-look deal at Alcon Entertainment, recalled that screenwriter/director LaGravenese and producer Erwin Stoff came to her early on, after initial discussions with Warner Bros. "Erwin and Richard brought it to [me], as a creative producer, and Alcon Entertainment to

> “ These movies are very broad in their appeal and, frankly, I think there's a wish-fulfillment aspect that transcends age. The idea of forbidden romance and finding the one love for you, combined with intrigues and fantasy elements, is very appealing. ”
>
> —**Andrew Kosove**, producer

All About Amma

Viola Davis as Amma.

For the adaptation from novel to film, the biggest change was the character of Amma. As in the novel, she would remain a seer, but LaGravenese's screenplay enfolded into her the attributes of Marian Ashcroft, a character in the novel who is the close friend of Ethan's late mother as well as the head librarian in Gatlin and the keeper of the secret Caster Library. "What works in a book might not work in a film," LaGravenese noted. The director felt he'd seen characters like Amma before on-screen. He wanted her to be unique. "And then I thought, *Well, why not make her the librarian and best friend of the mother?* So, she's not a housekeeper, but she's still like Ethan's second mother. I also thought that [a larger role] would attract a better actress. Viola was my only choice and the first person we cast."

"Viola was, literally, the only person discussed for the role," added producer Erwin Stoff. "But it just happened; we got lucky getting her. She was doing another movie that overlapped with ours, but she was shooting in New Orleans, so we were able to work out dates."

Davis, a Tony Award winner for *King Hedley II* and an Oscar nominee for *The Help*, had never heard of *Beautiful Creatures* before her manager and agent handed her the script and told her it was an interesting role for an African American woman. Although she had read and enjoyed the fantasy worlds of *Harry Potter* and *Twilight*, she acknowledged that scripts from that genre do not usually come her way. "I'm in the realistic world," she said with a chuckle. "After I signed on, my sister, who is a high school teacher, told me about the books, and she was so excited. It was then that I realized it had this huge fan base."

produce and finance the film. Richard and I have worked together previously, so we had a great relationship, as I produced *P.S. I Love You*, which he wrote and directed as well for Alcon. We all immediately loved *Beautiful Creatures* and took over the creative rights to make the film." LaGravenese would again write the screenplay and direct. Along with Stoff and Smith, the team included Alcon copresidents, cofounders, and co-CEOs Andrew Kosove and Broderick Johnson. Coming full circle, Warner Bros., which distributes Alcon's films, would release *Beautiful Creatures*—"a perfect fit," Smith concluded.

Kosove and Johnson agreed that the novel and Richard LaGravenese's take on the material were a winning combination. "*Beautiful Creatures* was ripe for a feature film because it had very compelling characters," noted Johnson. "It's not just about two young protagonists dealing with their romance, but also about real adult characters, and the mystery and history of this town. Richard LaGravenese is an extraordinary storyteller who has written some of the great screenplays in Hollywood. He knows character and storytelling, and those are the things that make a movie great. Richard bringing that level of talent to a piece like this was very compelling to us."

"At the end of the day, every filmmaker has to tell the story, and no one is better at story and character than Richard LaGravenese," Andrew Kosove agreed. "It was Richard's passion to tell not just a supernatural story, but a story that is really a metaphor for growing up and could be appealing to all ages. That's why we went forward on the project."

Director Richard LaGravenese shows the set to authors Kami Garcia and Margaret Stohl.

"What attracted me to *Beautiful Creatures* was the world and the core story," LaGravenese explained. "I wasn't thinking of the franchise, and I hadn't read the other books. I just wanted to tell this story the best I could. What I loved was the idea of the Claiming being sort of the metaphor for all of us, especially in our teens, when we have to individuate from our parents. That point of saying, 'This is who I am.' That idea, coupled with a love story, I found really interesting."

The authors first met LaGravenese at an early breakfast meeting in Charleston, a city that had been inspirational for the authors. (Ravenwood Manor, for instance, was inspired by the area's grand old plantation houses.) "He insisted on coming to Charleston to look at the location we had looked at when writing the book," Stohl recalled. "He was there with Erwin [Stoff], and we were on a book tour. Richard got out this little black book. He has this tiny handwriting, and he had a thousand questions. I was so impressed by his seriousness in his approach to our universe. It was never about parlaying someone's

(this page and opposite) Director Richard LaGravenese found inspiration on a tour of the South, particularly in McClellanville, South Carolina.

Photos courtesy Richard LaGravenese

teen franchise into something marketable. Richard is his own writer and an artist, and from the beginning was completely committed. It was truly built out of the story and the characters. We never really worried."

Producer Erwin Stoff described the production as being "on a fast track," with Alcon's Andrew Kosove and Broderick Johnson "very quick on the trigger. It was clear from the get-go that we were making the movie." The fifty days of principal photography would be based in New Orleans, a prime filmmaking venue due to the lure of tax incentives and local craftspersons and production crews.

The authors were consulted throughout but were happy to let the filmmakers work their magic. There was not much to object to when Emma Thompson was cast as Mrs. Lincoln, guardian of tradition and godliness in Gatlin, nor when Viola Davis signed on to play Amma, a role much expanded from the elderly African American housekeeper of the Wate household who practically raised Ethan after the passing of his mother and who is also a secret seer. The casting of Jeremy Irons as Macon Ravenwood, Caster and lord of Ravenwood Manor, held particular excitement for Kami Garcia; she swears the celebrated actor was always in her

Emma Thompson and Thomas Mann as the Lincolns.

mind when she was writing Macon. The young stars included Alden Ehrenreich as Ethan, Alice Englert as Lena, Thomas Mann as Link, and Emmy Rossum as Lena's Dark Caster cousin Ridley Duchannes.

LaGravenese, who refers to his "geek filmdom nature," brought to the production a love of movie history, and the images that might inspire a creative direction for his own film, coupled with a desire to give audiences something they had never seen before. The story was about magic and supernatural beings—Lena, for example, has the power to conjure dramatic weather events—but he wanted it all to look and feel real, not to be overwhelmed by computer-generated effects, and certainly not to look like a knockoff of the *Harry Potter* and *Twilight* films.

One of the production principals who would be key to realizing the director's vision was his director of photography, Philippe Rousselot, an Academy Award winner whose works range

(below) Setting up a shot from Ridley's car; (right) Alden Ehrenreich films a scene as Ethan Wate.

Alden Ehrenreich as Ethan Wate.

from Tim Burton's *Big Fish* (2003) and *Interview with the Vampire* (1994) to the recent *Sherlock Holmes* franchise. The production would shoot film using the anamorphic wide-screen format. "Philippe is a master cinematographer," LaGravenese said. "At our first meeting, I said to him that I didn't want this to be conventional. I didn't want to do, like television, over-the-shoulder shot after over-the-shoulder shot. I wanted to design elegant shots that could only be cut one way, using [conventional coverage] only in certain cases. And it was a wonderful collaboration. We had a lot of night sequences that would have been way too expensive on our budget, but he had wonderful ideas about using day for night that added a quality I liked very much." The relationship was very much about the director's staging and the cinematographer's aesthetic about light and camera angles. "I like depth and contrast. I like when it's a little bit messy, when things aren't so perfect. I love when an actor comes up with something, or the camera goes someplace you didn't expect it to. It gives life because it's spontaneous."

> "To tell this story in a coherent, believable, and dramatic way is the challenge of filming any novel. And to turn characters beloved by the reader into flesh and blood is always a task and responsibility not to be taken lightly."
>
> —**Jeremy Irons,** actor

Like many filmgoers of his generation, LaGravenese vividly recalls the impact of sitting in a darkened movie theater and watching William Friedkin's *The Exorcist*, the 1973 film about a troubled Catholic priest who tries to free a young girl of a demonic spirit that has possessed her. "I was fourteen when I saw *The Exorcist*, and one of those people traumatized by it," he admitted. For *A Decade Under the Influence*, the 2003 documentary on 1970s cinema that LaGravenese codirected and produced, he got to meet the man responsible. "We interviewed William Friedkin. And he said the reason he felt *The Exorcist* worked was that they weren't trying to make a horror movie. Everyone who worked on that movie *believed* it, believed in the reality of what they were doing."

LaGravenese wanted to bring such belief to the supernatural world of *Beautiful Creatures*. He acknowledged that when it came to visual effects, he was on a steep learning curve, but he didn't want story and character obscured by flashy CG (computer-generated) effects. "I think, on a subconscious level, audiences know it's fake. But the more you're grounded in character, then you can utilize visual effects and special effects to have a more organic, emotional reaction. Lena has power over the elements—earth, air, water, fire, and everything in between, what we're calling ether—and those effects should be organic; they should make sense."

Strangely, an effects veteran of such cutting-edge epics as *300*, *Avatar*, and *Hugo* coveted the position of visual effects supervisor for *Beautiful Creatures*. "I really, really, really wanted to work on this movie," Joe Harkins explained. "I just thought the script was so good. I didn't know Richard LaGravenese personally, but I knew of his work, more as a writer." Harkins had always worked on the "facility side"—that is, at the visual effects companies that a studio and production contracts with to execute specific shots. What he did for his job interview with the director and producers was, he admitted, risky—he came armed with two-D Photoshop artwork and animated drawings based on potential effects shots from the script.

"Usually you'd first have some creative discussion, brainstorm, and *then* show visuals," Harkins explained. "At that point you're feeling each other out. But I thought, *I've got nothing to lose, I'm going all out.* I hired a concept artist and spent hours working on Photoshop two-D and animated drawings. And I presented it to [LaGravenese] at the interview. One of the things was the concept of a fire effect that appears in the eyes of the Duchannes women. I took a photograph of a girl and, in a close-up, did a subtle integration of fire into her iris. Richard homed in on that, and that's the template for how we're doing that look in the final film. For me to communicate, on version one, with an idea he might have had somewhere in his brain meant we connected right away. I think that fire effect is what got me the job. This is my twenty-fourth film, but the first time I'm on the production side and supervising visual effects for the entire film."

The flipside of computer-generated visual effects imagery is special effects,

Costume designer Jeffrey Kurland's sketches for Lena, Aunt Del, and Gramma.

Sketches courtesy Jeffrey Kurland

Costume designer Jeffrey Kurland with several key costumes from the film.

the department that handles the "practical" shots created in live action for the camera. Special effects supervisor Matt Kutcher came to the production fresh off *Abraham Lincoln: Vampire Hunter* and would get the chance to stage more Civil War battle action for a flashback sequence that would be as key to the film as it was to the novel. "I sort it all out technically in my head to make sure the director's dream is realized the way he imagined it," explained Kutcher, whose company, Spectrum Effects, relocated from Hollywood to Louisiana two years ago. "We take the mechanics and mathematics into his head and marry the two."

Unit production manager Allen Kupetsky brought aboard many production principals, including makeup department head Fionagh Cush, whom he had worked with on *The Curious Case of Benjamin Button* (2008). Cush, a veteran of productions in New Orleans, had also come off *Abraham Lincoln: Vampire Hunter*. Joining her in the hair-and-makeup trailer was Terry Baliel, whose recent credits include *In Time* (2011), *Inception* (2010), and *Alice in Wonderland* (2010). Both departments would follow the lead of the costume designer in helping the actors bring their characters to life. "In most movies, the costume designer decides what everyone is really going to look like," Baliel explained. "A great costume designer, like Jeffrey Kurland, is very open to your ideas, and you bounce things back and forth until you find an end result that you're all satisfied with."

Costume designer Jeffrey Kurland, another veteran of *Inception*, had a core crew of seven to eight people, with at least three on set every day. The team included Kurland's assistant and supervisor, a cutter and fitter, three seamstresses, designers in New York and Los Angeles making clothes for the principal actors, and agers and dyers working throughout filming to distress every piece of clothing. ("Nothing ever goes in front of the camera looking as if it just came out of a box," Kurland noted.)

Production designer Richard Sherman's department included art director Lorin Flemming and supervising art director Troy Sizemore, with construction coordinator Randy Coe building the final approved sets. They had all come straight from the final *Breaking Dawn* chapters of the Twilight Saga. Sherman himself had been enjoying a break in October 2011 when he was presented with *Beautiful Creatures*. "I liked Richard LaGravenese as a writer, and I liked *Living Out Loud* [the 1998 film that LaGravenese wrote and that also marked his directorial debut]. I knew nothing about *Beautiful Creatures*, and I was reluctant to do it. . . . But, obviously, I did do it and had a good time doing it. It was very challenging."

Sherman was on board in late December 2011, with Lorin Flemming arriving in New Orleans in January to start preproduction work. "I really liked the script," said Flemming. "It was a great Southern gothic romance, plus the supernatural elements, and there were a lot of exciting sets to build."

The hair department affixes a headdress to a Caster Ball guest.

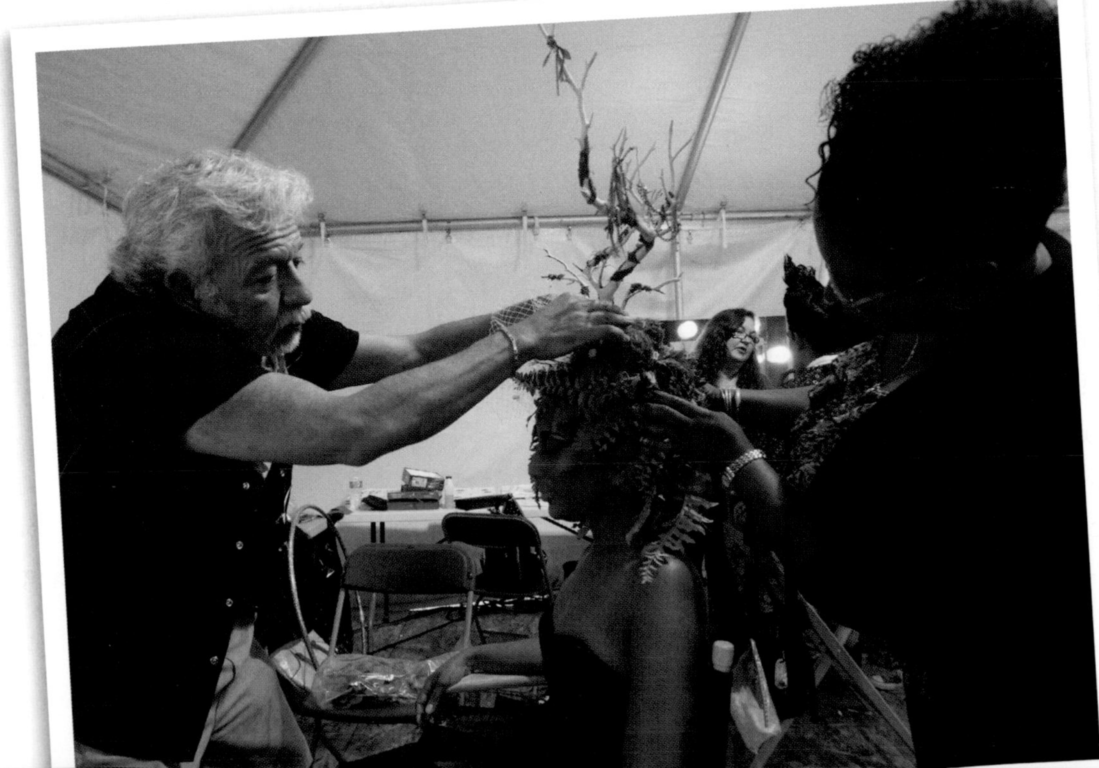

The production would discover that although LaGravenese was both writer and director, he did not consider his screenplay sacred text. During filming, things could change, sometimes suddenly. "The script was a nice love story, with flashbacks to the Civil War," Cush recalled. "But it became bigger than the love story and was not how myself and Terry Baliel read the first draft of the script. It definitely got more involved, with more makeup. Every day the director asked, 'Can we do *this*?' And once things started rolling, it was great to give him everything he wanted. My core crew was Carla Chao Brenholzt and Kim Perrodin. This doesn't include artists I used on the Civil War and the Caster party. We had a lot to cover in what ended up as a big production."

Baliel also thought the shoot would be simple and straightforward after reading the script. "Then it turned into a movie that was all about wigs," he said. "For example, Emmy Rossum plays a Caster, or a witch, who transforms herself to suit her needs. So every time she wanted to seduce somebody or play games, her look changed radically. She required five different wigs for seven different looks throughout the film." Baliel had outside vendors make the custom wigs: Bob Kretschmer did Emmy Rossum's wigs, and Natascha of Favian Wigs in Woodland Hills made wigs for actress Margo Martindale, who played Lena's aunt Del, with additional work by Alex Rouse and Carol Waugh in London. (Waugh made a wig for Eileen Atkins, who plays Lena's grandmother, but a wig she'd made for Irons was not used, as, ultimately, the actor's own hair would be styled for the film.)

"EVERY DAY THE DIRECTOR ASKED, 'CAN WE DO *THIS*?'"

The hairstyling was just one detail that became more complex in the transition from script to production. "A script is a blueprint," LaGravenese noted. "Scripts are not meant to be read—they are meant to be made into movies! A script, of course, has the story and characters. But if I could work with my actors and add another layer to it, that was so much the better. I was lucky with my entire cast and crew. They didn't want to make something derivative. Even though it was this magical world, we all wanted to make something original that felt real, and everyone helped contribute to that. And if that meant cutting down or rewriting lines, or coming up with more ideas, that's what we did."

Early in 2012, the production began heading to Louisiana and the Big Easy to get ready for filming. "New Orleans

"SCRIPTS ARE NOT MEANT TO BE READ—
THEY ARE MEANT TO BE MADE INTO MOVIES!"

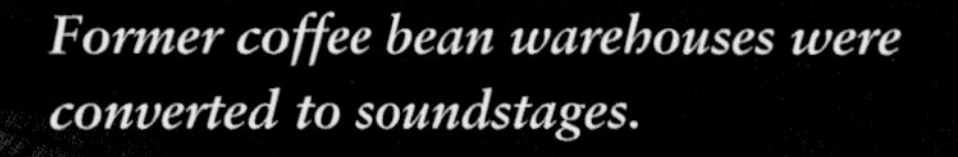

Former coffee bean warehouses were converted to soundstages.

has been dubbed the Hollywood of the South," said *Beautiful Creatures* stunt coordinator Chuck Picerni Jr. "I moved to New Orleans about two years ago and hit the ground running. Once people found out I was down there, the phone started ringing."

The downside was that a lot of shows were already there and competing for local resources. "The crew was very hard to come by because there were a lot of things shooting in New Orleans and that area at that time, so we had a very limited staff," Baliel explained. "We only had, at most, five or six people on all our big days to do all this work. So it was a little hard sometimes because we had very limited manpower. My assistant and key hairstylist, Tony Ward, was fabulous. I couldn't have done the film without him. A lot of the time your key takes over and runs the department for you, under your jurisdiction, so you're free to do the design and prep work, and he was great about that. And he had a great personality for the [hair-and-makeup] trailer. He was low-key and calm, which was good because there was a lot of chaos trying to scramble and get everything done."

The production's main stages were across the Mississippi River from New Orleans, in the town of Algiers. "We had our soundstages in warehouses that, previous to us, hosted millions of bags of coffee beans," Lorin Flemming said with a smile. "They emptied them out for us, and we converted as best we could, but it reeked of coffee beans the whole time. It's funny, because in LA there are hundreds of beautiful soundstages sitting empty, while we're converting soundstages everywhere else."

"We were lucky to find it, given how busy New Orleans was," said producer Molly Smith. "It was a fantastic, huge stage space. We had [interior sets] in which a lot of action took place, and we needed to be able to move around inside. We built the interior of Ravenwood onstage, the bedrooms of Lena and Ethan, and the interior of the incredible Caster Library. I definitely think the whole process is a bit of magic. It's a lot of work, and challenging, and a constant battle between art and logistics. But when you solve the puzzle and it all comes together with an incredible team of talented individuals, it's an amazing experience."

CHAPTER 2

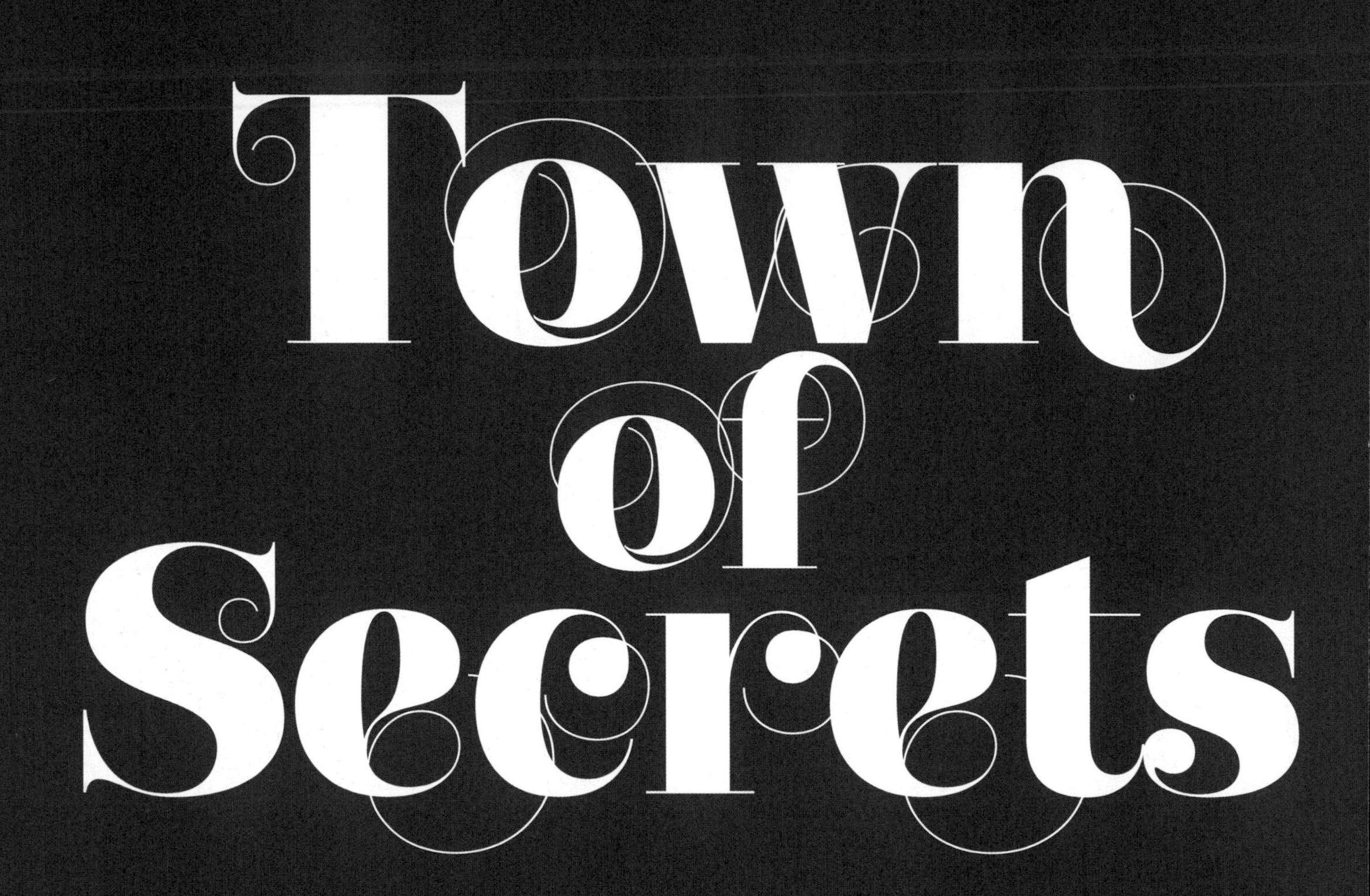

“I always love movies that show a world behind a world. Everything looks perfectly normal, but it’s explained to you in ways you’ve never seen or thought of before. This film has that aspect. It’s about the supernatural, but that’s woven in with the real world.”

—Ewrin Stoff, producer

While filming in the South meant that the production would struggle with Louisiana's notorious heat and humidity, as well as bugs and snakes, it also meant the filmmakers would breathe in the very atmosphere of the world they were creating.

"That whole area is haunted," said supervising art director Troy Sizemore, who has lived in New Orleans. "I mean, they bury people aboveground. There are a lot of old souls floating around Louisiana, for sure. It's a fascinating and rich historical place.... It all seems very spiritually disturbed and unsettled. I've seen ghosts there. My roommate and I lived in the Quarter and had a third-floor balcony. We both saw this older gentleman in a butler's outfit come floating through from off the balcony, and he was there more than once. [The ghost] might have come from across the street, a place that had been a kind of torture chamber.... It's on one of the tours of the Quarter, where they stop carriages and tell you about it.

"Even though this was written for South Carolina, Louisiana lent itself to the story. I've done films in New Orleans that pretended to be Chicago or New York or Los Angeles or some place, and it doesn't make sense, but you're doing it anyway. Doing this story there made sense. It belonged there, in a way."

The fictional town of Gatlin is the

al moment for Ethan (Alden Ehrenreich) na (Alice Englert).

"GATLIN WAS GATLIN. . . . WE WERE PRETTY MUCH THE EPICENTER OF THE MIDDLE OF NOWHERE."

A "prop" for the production—the sign on the way out of Gatlin.

most uncomplicated and predictable of places, as Ethan Wate attests in the novel: "Gatlin was Gatlin. . . . We were pretty much the epicenter of the middle of nowhere."[3] Kids like Ethan might carry iPods, but they are stuck in the drowsy rhythm of bygone times. Ethan's family has abided in Gatlin for generations, but he longs to be rid of the place. His mother is dead, and his still-grieving father is locked away in his study. But life for Ethan changes with the arrival of Lena Duchannes, the new girl in town who lives with her uncle, Macon Ravenwood, in the creepy old plantation house the locals shun. Lena leads Ethan into a world of Casters and adventures he never imagined.

"It seemed logical to set our story in the South because it's a place full of superstition and magic," Kami Garcia noted. "If you visit cities like New Orleans, Charleston, and Savannah, you can sense it. The houses are incredibly old and date back to the Revolutionary and Civil Wars. Generation after generation have lived in them, and people have died in them—and *for* them. There's just a different sensibility.

"And 'crazy' is more expected in the South—you walk your crazy down the street, proud. It was an awesome place to have Lena and Casters, because where else could a magical race hide out and not be noticed than among people who are incredibly quirky? But in our

" Gatlin is, essentially, a peaceful small town that is terrified of the strange and unknown while actually being *full* of the strange. It's a place where prejudice, violence, and manipulation prevail under the guise of manners and simplicity. "

—**Alice Englert,**
actor

Jeremy Irons as Macon Ravenwood.

small town there's also the insular, conservative piece we wanted. You could be crazy, but you can't come in and be *different*. You have to get with the program or keep it to yourself."

Garcia and Stohl had dreamed up the term *Casters*, which they derived from "spell casters." "We wanted to create our own mythology," Garcia explained. "Casters are a combination of witches and superheroes, but they don't share a universal set of powers like witches. Each Caster is born with a distinct set of powers, and there are different types of Casters. We did use some traditional mythology for certain Casters, like Lena's cousin Ridley, who is a siren with the power of persuasion. In other cases, the mythology was a starting point. Macon Ravenwood is an incubus, but I did research and discovered that some cultures have stories about incubuses who come in the night and affect people's dreams. But in every instance, they had a parasitic nature, so we made Macon into a supernatural who is strong and fast, almost like a vampire, but feeds off dreams."

A few souls in Gatlin know of the Casters, notably Amma. "There are a couple people, like Carlton Eaton, who delivers the mail, who know about the Casters," Garcia revealed, "but it's not widespread knowledge. The few who know Casters exist don't discuss it. It's really a magical world hidden in plain sight.

Jeffrey Kurland's sketches for Macon's costumes.

Sketches courtesy Jeffrey Kurland

"There's a different sensibility in a small town. We changed a persecution of race to a persecution of difference. In our universe it began with outsiders, then moves on to Casters. Whether it's racial or religious or sexual orientation, there are people being pushed to the fringes because they don't fit into the mainstream."

The town of Gatlin wasn't built—it was found. "We shot in a lot of beautiful small towns outside New Orleans, like Covington and Saint Francisville, to create Gatlin," producer Molly Smith said. "The look of the town

" The process of working out the looks of all the characters started right at the beginning with Richard, the director and also the writer, which was a very, very lucky break when you're making a movie like this. The character studies were kind of discussed and figured out before we had a cast. "

—Jeffrey Kurland,
costume designer

“Richard [LaGravenese] kept saying, ‘Do not make the witches look ugly; I want them to look like beautiful creatures.’ He said, ‘If I was a witch, I wouldn’t make myself look ugly, so I don’t want anyone to look ugly in this movie. I want them to look different.’ That was always in the back of our minds: *Make them look beautiful.*”

—**Fionagh Cush**,
makeup department head

The family at the Caster Ball.

is old-fashioned, with a lot of gorgeous Spanish moss trees that helped create atmosphere. Our production designer, Richard Sherman, did a wonderful job finding old plantations and locations where we shot practically, and we built a lot of the interiors on a stage.”

“Gatlin is a fictitious town, but it’s supposed to be near Charleston,” Sherman explained. “Covington, across from Lake Pontchartrain, had all the elements we needed for a town that once looked nice. The irony is that Covington is a wealthy community, with beautiful houses and restaurants. But we found this little stretch that had a depressed look and rusted old warehouses outside town. Most of the store windows were emptied out because they were out of business. It added fuel to Ethan wanting to get out, but the poor kid is stuck here. He’s smart, he likes to read, he is interesting and, more importantly, *interested*, and this is not the place for this guy—until he runs into Lena.”

The exterior of the Wate residence would be a house found on location, while Ethan’s bedroom was a set built on the production’s warehouse stage. “Ethan is very much into literature and [a desire for] traveling, so his room reflected that,” art director Lorin Flemming explained. “There are a lot of great descriptions in the book about this map he has marked with places he wants to visit that relate to books he’s read. It’s an attic room, so it had a great feel to it, and that lent itself to a certain look. There was an interesting window in the attic of the house on location, so we also incorporated that into the interior set."

Although *Beautiful Creatures* prop master Brook Yeaton provided the "standard" items for Ethan's schoolmates—schoolbooks, backpacks, rings, watches, and sunglasses—the personal effects for Ethan were unique to him. Because he's a reader, Ethan's bedroom bookshelves included such offbeat classics as *A Clockwork Orange* and *The Catcher in the Rye* (copies of which Yeaton's department had to find and then have cleared before being able to use). The prop master had also noticed a reference in the script for a keepsake box of Ethan's that held family photos and trinkets. "Ethan's keepsake box had little toy soldiers, marbles, a jack for playing jacks, the little compass that used to come in Cracker Jack boxes—anything we could come across that had that feel," Yeaton said. "It was fun to do."

Alden Ehrenreich noted that he didn't film his scenes in Ethan's bedroom until the end of filming. But he enjoyed hanging out in his character's attic room, if only to read some of the great books on Ethan's bookshelves. "The room was crafted with painstaking detail and was a really magical place. I told Richard Sherman that the moment I walked into my room set, it felt as if all the work I had done on my character

Alden Ehrenreich and Alice Englert pose for photos together.

❝ When Ethan meets Lena, he meets someone who has a more sophisticated and deeper point of view, and her own emotional tumult involving family. Lena is unafraid to speak her mind and voice her attitudes and experiences. This is what Ethan has been looking for. What he thought he would only find 'on the road,' or in some marvelous new city or country, he finds in a person who shares a lot of the restlessness and anxiousness he has, and they help mend each other's broken heart. ❞

—**Alden Ehrenreich**, actor

suddenly took this physical form. It was like a reward. I finally realized my vision of Ethan. He craves adventure, he wants to have experiences he knows don't happen in this small town. Because of his mother's death, he is driven by emotions that live uncomfortably inside him. He wants to be somewhere else, where those emotions can take shape. Gatlin is very small-minded and repressive. 'People think it was God's will she died' is what Ethan says about the townspeople."

As far as physically becoming their characters, the two young leads already looked their parts. Custom wigs were used for many of the principal performers, but Alden Ehrenreich and Alice Englert used their own hair. "We just darkened it up," Terry Baliel explained. "Alice had sort of blondish-brownish hair, and we felt it would be more in character if it was darker and richer. Later, there's a party for her Claiming, and for that we added hair extensions—a row of hair we clip in to add body and length—because she was becoming a woman, so to speak, and we wanted her hair to appear richer and more lush."

The costume designer took a subtle hand in showing Ethan and Lena growing closer as they begin falling in love. "At the beginning, Ethan looks like another kid in school, whereas Lena doesn't look like anybody in the school," Jeffrey Kurland said. "Ethan wears jeans and sneakers, short-sleeve shirts with a hint of a Western touch, with snaps in front and such. We kept him in the darker tone range, with some greens. But there's logic to him and Lena being together, and you see a link as the film progresses. Hopefully, it doesn't hit you over the head, but you'll see the tones [of their wardrobes] are flattering for each other and sort of meld together. By the end there's a comfortable symbiosis.

"Lena is a loner—she's on her own and she's lived most of her life that way," Kurland continued. "By her very nature she's different from kids her age, and has never been able to make friends. So her look and fashion sense is individual to her. I used a lot of vintage clothing to give her a little more sophistication, and she wears darker tones than the other kids [do]. She favors boots and flatter shoes; she's not wearing

In the movie, as in the novel, Ethan (Alden Ehrenreich) is an avid reader.

Ethan (Alden Ehrenreich) and Lena (Alice Englert).

heels all the time. She wears jeans once as a practicality, but mostly it's skirts and dresses and interesting found items from a vintage store. It's all very textural, and there are layers of things. She will wear lace over silk, so you get the texture of the lace on top and a bit of sheen underneath. She'll wear a sweater over a vintage blouse, or a vintage jacket over a blouse. Lena is much more into solid fabrics and darker tones. She doesn't wear patterns, like the other girls in school, that look you see in the South in younger girls trying to emulate their mothers."

The makeup, particularly for Lena and her fellow Casters, avoided any resemblance to the pale-faced vampires of the Twilight Saga. "One big fear our director had was they had to look unearthly but not vampiric," Fionagh Cush explained. "So we couldn't make them pale. Both Alice Englert and Alden Ehrenreich are extremely pale, so we had to warm Alden up a bit. Alice is a very young, beautiful girl, so I didn't put too much tan on her, knowing she is our witch character. She looks sweet and plain, but as we progress and get nearer the date of her Claiming, we wanted to make her look stronger. In particular, the director really wanted her eyes to look more intense. He liked black kohl around her eyes, which is very hip and trendy now. It looked great, but keeping it neat and not smudgy was a nightmare—the second you walk out in that humidity, everything kind of melts. That was the biggest challenge. It was constant maintenance, all day long."

Cush emphasized that it was vital to be at the first wardrobe fittings, or send someone to take pictures, because that's where the process started. "You don't want any surprises. The actors get fitted and you see what wardrobe is going to put them in. And then, with hair, we all work together. During production you want to keep the chairs moving in the makeup-and-hair trailer; you don't ever want to be sitting around waiting on somebody. So you figure out if hair needs to put a wig on an actor first, or whether they need to come to makeup first."

Although his role was one of the leads, Ehrenreich was cast late in the process and he didn't come onto the production until a week before filming. It was as if Ethan Wate had been prepared and made ready for him, like a tailored suit to slip into. The wardrobe, hair, makeup, props, and other departments "had spent a lot more time crafting their vision of my character than I had, which was a new experience for me. So I felt I could learn from them because their view of Ethan was more sophisticated than mine. I spent the first week 'cramming for the test,' so to speak."

"Alden and Alice are accomplished and dedicated young actors, who are very generous," producer Erwin Stoff noted. "The chemistry between them was evident from the first time they met. Alden't late entry into the cast was not a concern."

> "What attracted me to Lena was her humanity. Despite her supernatural nature, I thought she had all the complications, nuance, and passion of a young woman dealing with emotions that feel too large and out of control. She faces persecution [and] prejudice, and she falls in love. I liked her struggles. It's a haunting coming-of-age story."
>
> —**Alice Englert**, actor

Gatlin includes an ultraconservative faction led by Emma Thompson's Mrs. Lincoln, who is the mother of Ethan's best friend, Link (played by Thomas Mann). Mrs. Lincoln is the scourge of the outsider girl, Lena. "Mrs. Lincoln and her 'posse,' as we called them, are conservative types who wear religion on their sleeve," Kurland noted. "For my research for Emma's character, I went into the fifties, sixties, and seventies to see what women of a conservative bent wore, as well as a very American style. So you see her in things like a housedress. But when she goes out, she dresses to go out. She never wears pants; she always wears dresses and skirts. There's a throwback to a fifties and sixties sensibility. I think certain women lock into a choice of

(left) Emma Thompson as Mrs. Lincoln; (inset) Mrs. Lincoln stages a protest at the high school.

clothing and hairstyle and stick to it, and Mrs. Lincoln is one of those women. She's very proper; there's a primness to her."

"It was very much a question of getting the accent right," Thompson said. "Mrs. Lincoln herself is a victim of circumstances—bad education, lack of opportunity, and a certain obsessive-compulsiveness.... My accent coach, Rick Lipton, was hugely influential in helping me to understand the emotions under the voice. And of course our costume designer, the extraordinary Jeffrey Kurland, couldn't wait to get me into a dowdy housecoat on the one hand, and a gigantic Southern belle outfit on the other."

Mrs. Lincoln leads a crusade against Lena and her family, decrying them as devil worshippers. But Lena is also tormented by a clique of girls at the high school led by Emily Asher. It certainly doesn't help Lena's cause that Emily sees

> "The most challenging aspect [of filming] was the heat and humidity. It's difficult enough to breathe, but when you add a very tight corset, things start to get interesting."
>
> —**Emma Thompson**, actor

herself losing her old boyfriend, Ethan, to this oddball outsider.

Emily Asher was the first movie role for seventeen-year-old actress Zoey Deutch. "The second I got the part, I dyed my hair a bright shade of honey blond and ran straight to the nail salon for some shiny pink acrylics, or, as I call them, 'Emily's claws,'" Deutch said.

"My biggest challenge was finding ways to not judge Emily Asher," she admitted. "I think it's important to understand the person you're playing as best you can, but with Emily's fervent opinions and the ruthless bullying, it was difficult at the beginning. Emily is the most popular girl in school, but probably the most insecure, too—she has a lot of layers, and that's why she was so fun to play. She has her heart broken by Ethan and doesn't know how to channel her pain, which is why she develops such a hard shell. Anger and pain always come from a deeper place, and the authors of *Beautiful Creatures* and Richard LaGravenese did a wonderful job of showing her broken heart underneath

(top to bottom) Best friends Ethan (Alden Ehrenreich) and Link (Thomas Mann); Lena and Ethan's classmates (Tiffany Boone, Morgan Lirette, and Zoey Deutch) take photos of an unusual local phenomenon; (left) Emily Asher (Zoey Deutch) flirts with Ethan.

Lena (Alice Englert) quickly becomes an outcast at school.

all her cruelty toward others. However, when I got to know her better, I discovered she's a normal teenage girl who realizes the person she's in love with doesn't care about her anymore. Heartbreak can make the strongest venom."

Deutch prepared for her big break by reading the script over and over and making notes throughout—"I wrote so many notes I could barely see the lines [of the screenplay]," she said—and she even attended religious services at an evangelical church to give her insights into the religious community that would be prevalent in Gatlin, South Carolina.

"Once I got to New Orleans, I was excited to find that wardrobe didn't just go the stereotypical cheerleader route—Emily was church conservative with a touch of sexy preppy with a little cowgirl; contradictory and complicated, just like she is. My favorite parts were the embroidered cowboy boots and heeled sandals, which helped me walk in a different way than I normally do. . . . I honestly just tried to go with my instincts and pull from what I've learned working on different TV shows. The hair and nails absolutely helped me take that first step into feeling like Emily."

Despite her tormentors in school and out, Lena still wants to have friends and be accepted, but she grows apprehensive as her fateful sixteenth birthday approaches. As if she needed a reminder, a magical tattoo on her hand keeps changing as the days tick down. The makeup department made and applied the tattoos, and Cush worked with the script supervisor to figure out which date to prepare for a given scene. "With the script supervisor, we worked out maybe ten different dates. Since we jumped around from scene to scene during filming, that tattoo had to come off three or four times a day to reflect the correct date. When Ethan first sees the tattoo, she pulls her hand away. But he notices the number has changed. He doesn't understand what's supposed to happen until she tells him."

The actors, director, cinematographer, costume, hair, makeup, props—Ethan and Lena's relationship was shaped and guided by a collaborative effort. But how it all ultimately played out on-screen would fall to LaGravenese and his editor, David Moritz. Usually characterized as postproduction, the editorial side had to be hands-on from the moment the first piece of film ran through the camera. "When you have relationships with directors—this is my third film with Rich—I go to the film's location," Moritz explained. "You get a more organic feel for the movie while being on set. I see what Rich is going for, and we have time to look at dailies, which are the rushes of the day's footage."

> "Gatlin is a painful culmination of the reality that is so many high schools. Truthfully, 'cool' kids, 'uncool' kids, and everyone in between all feel scared and confused. How these kids try to combat those feelings in adolescence varies from character to character."
>
> —**Zoey Deutch**, actor

Lena's (Alice Englert) tattoos are touched up by a makeup artist on set.

The fun of editing included the ability to change the dynamics of time, space, and even reality, according to Moritz. "A scene takes on more significance because of what's going on around it, or because you have built up to that moment. For us, there are a lot of moments with Lena and Ethan where all this chaos is happening around them and, suddenly, you slow down and zoom in on them. You always want to make sure their story is what you're locked into; you want to pay attention to what a character is *seeing*. By doing so, an audience, whether they realize it or not, is witnessing what's happening in any given scene through the eyes of

Ethan (Alden Ehrenreich) and Lena (Alice Englert) hop the wall to wander the grounds of the Greenbrier plantation; (inset) the Duchannes vault set.

that character. Rather than just being a viewer, you're sort of in the character's experience. That's what we always strive for, at least in this particular movie. Hopefully, Ethan and Lena represent what all kids go through when they feel conflicted. The audience realizes, 'He's feeling that because *I'm* feeling that.'"

To escape an ignorant world and uncomprehending adults, Ethan and Lena find refuge and retreat in the wild ruins of Greenbrier, a former plantation next to Ravenwood Manor that had been burned down during the Civil War. Greenbrier inspired another movie reference from the director, this time the opening of David O. Selznick and Alfred Hitchcock's *Rebecca* (1940). " 'Last night I dreamt I went to Manderley again,'" art director Flemming intoned, recalling the opening narration and vision of a mysterious, magnificent ruin. "The moon kind of shines through these old ruins, and it looks like people are there, but you realize it's just the shell of an old house. Whenever Richard had something in mind, he usually had something from a film he could relate to us, a great visual place to go."

Through the magic of the Internet,

Flemming came up with blueprints for old plantations, along with photographic references and books on plantation ruins. The location set would also include an overgrown, pre–Civil War family cemetery with nearly thirty headstones and a "hero" mausoleum flanked by mythic-looking caryatids sculpted by art department sculptor Brent Barnidge.

The tall and broken columns and chunks of crumbling wall were built from foam intricately carved by the sculpting department, then hard-coated and painted. The set was built to come apart and be put back together—the art director called it a "jigsaw puzzle"—and transported by truck to the woodlands of Folsom, north of Lake Pontchartrain. "We built it in the shop because you wouldn't want to carve foam out in nature; it would get everywhere," explained supervising art director Troy Sizemore. "The location was hot and buggy, with poison ivy and snakes, but it was beautiful. We wanted to keep it pristine and looking like nobody had been walking through it, which is difficult when you have a construction project."

Sizemore and construction coordinator Randy Coe managed to find a "dead side," a back way into the field, and policed the site to keep it as untouched as possible. Coe's construction crew used giant forklifts and huge booms to bring in the set pieces—some columns were as big as forty feet, by Sizemore's estimates. The columns had a cable down the middle that allowed them to be tightened into the ground for more stability. "Randy and Troy spearheaded

The outdoor set created for the ruins of Greenbrier.

The historical locket that shows Ethan and Lena visions of the past.

the creation of these pathways for the trucks and Condors and stuff to go through," Flemming noted. "The team was really amazing, and we maintained the integrity of this beautiful field the whole time."

A strange locket that Ethan has discovered provides the magical key by which he and Lena open the secrets of Greenbrier and the curse surrounding Genevieve Duchannes, revealed as one of Lena's Civil War–era ancestors. "The locket triggers a whole flashback sequence," prop master Yeaton explained. "The locket basically ties everything together and is a pivotal piece in the script. It's a common thread throughout generations of this family."

When it came to the key talisman, the prop master did what prop masters do—he went shopping. "I did research on Civil War–era lockets, then shopped a lot of antiques stores in New Orleans and on eBay, which is a great place to shop for props. I bought a lot of lockets and put them in a row. I then took a lot of different elements and put them in one." After final clearances and approvals, the final design was a sunburst with filigree between the stylized rays. The original locket and duplicates were molded and made under Yeaton's direction by an LA prop company, the Hand Prop Room.

Ethan and Lena discover that when they both touch the locket, the fabric of time splits open, revealing visions of Genevieve and the Civil War. One such jolting vision occurs when they go to see a movie. "We wanted a run-down, old deco movie theater," Flemming said, "a weathered and worn movie theater." The art department found an old theater, or what was left of one. Except for the marquee that inexplicably remained, the place had been gutted and transformed into condos. In place of the box-office ticket booth and lobby entrance was a big iron door that slid open to a parking area. It was still used, with a facade built around the existing marquee, providing the illusion of the movie theater it once was.

To David Moritz, the vision Ethan and Lena share in the theater was a

“Every part of the process, from pre- to postproduction, is essential to the final product, and every choice is influential to our story. Wardrobe and makeup were an important ritual in finding the character. During prep for Lena, I would pretend that the erratic weather of New Orleans was my own doing.”

—**Alice Englert**, actor

perfect example of what he called "the *Beautiful Creatures* sensibility."

"The idea is that if you peel things back, there's an alternate reality. It's otherworldly, like how you can clearly see a remembered dream in your head. What they see is not 'real,' but it appears to be, and it affects them emotionally. So in the movie theater they're watching this movie, and when they touch the locket together, this flashback happens. They become incorporated into this other reality happening around them in the theater. They're not watching a flashback on the movie screen, and it's something only they are experiencing. It's a hugely ambitious idea to take on."

"I have to admit there is part of me that believes in the supernatural world," LaGravenese said. "There's the idea that all time is happening simultaneously, and certain people can see that. One of the ideas of this film is that magic can pierce that veil at certain times."

It would fall to visual effects supervisor Joe Harkins to help realize the magical elements of that idea. "The Greenbrier flashbacks were a really complex idea," Harkins said. "It's like a dream sequence where images appear

Ethan (Alden Ehrenreich) offers Lena (Alice Englert) a ride in the rain.

together on top of each other and dissolve, and there are superimpositions and double-exposed images. This is one of those things we had to plan very carefully, including how we would shoot it for real. It's a little easier to figure out what a storm should look like than this implied idea of magic. They didn't want to be like *Harry Potter* and *Twilight*. But at the same time, you do have to look to something."

Richard LaGravenese had plenty of cinematic references for his visual effects supervisor, including Jean Cocteau's 1946 film *Beauty and the Beast*, with its enchanted castle realized with such sublime effects as a shadowy hallway lined with human arms holding candelabrums. He also showed the cast a ghost story—*The Innocents*, the 1961 film version of Henry James's *The Turn of the Screw*—that created its eerie atmosphere with camera work, staging, and performance, not visual effects.

"Richard's mind works a little differently; he's an encyclopedia of movies," Harkins said. "I've had an education from him, watching older films that didn't have any visual effects at all but still had cool stuff happening. It's like people forget what was done. They move on and try something new, and everything ends up looking bland and the same. There was a lot of originality and these freaky moments back then. Richard pulls from that; he references things from the past. Richard was trying to get across the simplicity in being able to tell a scary moment without overloading the visual effects. [That was] the irony for my job, and he said this in front of me all the time: 'I want to make a visual effects movie that is *not* visual effects–driven, that is character-driven.' We'd have journalists come on set, and he would tell them that, and they'd look completely baffled. But that's his approach—tell the story first."

CHAPTER 3

Macon's Whim

> In the *Beautiful Creatures* novel, the exterior of Ravenwood looks very overgrown and old and worn down.... We used that idea in the movie as well. On the outside it looks like one thing, but it has a completely incongruous interior... because magic people with supernatural powers live there.

—Richard LaGravenese, director

It's an iconic feature of every archetypal small town—the house of mystery. Ravenwood Manor, a Greek Revival–style plantation house, once might have been grand, but now it has pretty much gone to seed. The paint has long since peeled off its Doric columns; the sloping roof gives the impression the house is "leaning over like an arthritic old woman"; the crumbling front porch seems ready to slip from tenuous moorings; and thick ivy has a stranglehold on the walls and windows.[4]

The interiors of Ravenwood were realized as sets at the warehouse stage. The production wanted an actual house for the exterior view, but production designer Richard Sherman didn't want the typical plantation estate. "Richard [LaGravenese] had never done a movie in the South, but he has *seen* a lot of movies from the South," Sherman said. "I wanted to pull him away from that world of Greek Revival plantation house with big white columns. I wanted to try to find something a little more unique."

The location scouts fanned out beyond New Orleans and found an old house in Batchelor, a little place where the nearest town with stores and shops was Morganza. The house was owned

The exterior of Ravenwood Manor—an actual house that was painted and dressed with prop vines.

by "a man who doesn't really live there," Sherman recalled, a noted artist who spent most of his time at his studio in New York City. What Sherman discovered when he first visited the location was an old house with its own atmosphere of intrigue and mystery. Although the production designer never met the owner, Sherman had heard that a ghost had told the man to buy the place, so he did.

"It didn't look remotely like the antebellum style," Sherman recalled. "It was pre–Civil War, probably built in the 1820s, and surrounded by trees with moss. It was a very odd-looking house with big, tall windows and doors, columns made of wrought iron, [and] a big porch that wrapped around the whole house, and it was painted a kind of dusty rose. I loved it, this rosy-colored house with the green and trees and moss all around. We saw a lot of other places,

"I knew Richard LaGravenese and his people were talented and that they had amazing actors. But the sets, the props, the details that went into building the rooms of Ravenwood, the wardrobe for someone like Macon, this worldly gentleman—it exceeded my expectations. Ravenwood was the first set we saw, and it was shocking to walk in and see this staircase and foyer. The exterior was this beautiful plantation home that they aged and covered with dust, with a crooked porch and these overgrown grounds and vines and ivy growing up all over the place....The details they took from the book, and the level of detail, were insane."

—**Kami Garcia**, author

but we ended up using it. The art department came in and covered the whole house with vines, the way it's described in the script. The one battle I lost was Richard *hated* [the dusty rose color]. He just would not have it. So we painted it with a wash, which was fine.

"Inside, the place is jammed with hundreds of years' worth of art collections, antique furniture, huge crystal chandeliers, tapestries, carpets, and big, elaborate draperies with long fringe.

❝ It was very emotional when we showed up on the Ravenwood set with Julie Scheina, our editor. We're staring at Jeremy Irons dressed in a smoking jacket, looking more like Macon Ravenwood than even Macon did, and he was speaking with his pitch-perfect accent and moving like a cat as he's scanning the middle of this Ravenwood set that was so perfectly, lovingly rendered, right down to every detail. We all were so blown away. ❞

—**Margaret Stohl**, author

The interior of Ravenwood Manor.

Jeremy Irons, Alice Englert, and Alden Ehrenreich on the interior set of Ravenwood, which was built in a warehouse stage.

Remember the sweeping staircase of the big house that Rhett and Scarlett move into at the end of *Gone with the Wind*? It looked like that! I said, 'My God, the family [that must have lived here for generations]. But there was no family. There was no lineage. This artist followed what the ghost suggested and had bought an empty house and furnished it to look the way it looks now. There was even a moment when we said, 'Should we [film inside]?' But I've shot in old plantation houses before. On one hand they're sturdy, but they're also fragile and can't really handle the wear and tear from grips coming in and setting up equipment, and so much stuff happens in Ravenwood that we'd have to be inside the house for a long time. So it was better to build the interior."

Ethan first meets the lord of the manor when he works up the nerve to come to Ravenwood to see Lena. "When we first see Macon, he's on the front porch of the house," Jeffrey Kurland recalled. "He's in a relaxed mood, wearing a dressing gown with lounging clothes underneath. He looks extremely elegant, in a Cary Grant–ish way—but there's a real mystery to him."

Brook Yeaton held a character prop "show and tell" with each actor, laying out personal items for their characters, with options (such as ten Salvation Army Bibles for Emma Thompson to

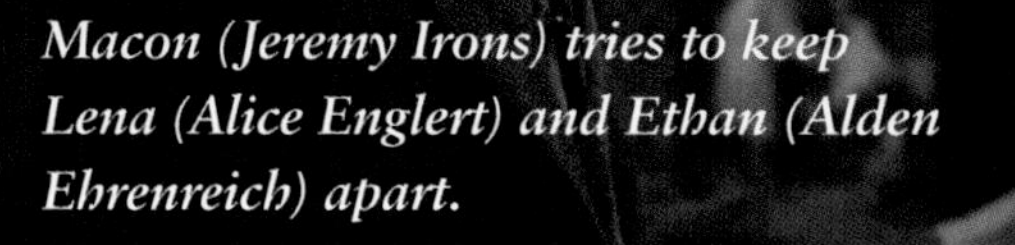

Macon (Jeremy Irons) tries to keep Lena (Alice Englert) and Ethan (Alden Ehrenreich) apart.

consider for the Bible-thumping Mrs. Lincoln), but Irons did not want the usual personal items, with one exception. "For the scene where we introduce him, he wanted a hardcover reprint book of *MAD* magazine, with Alfred E. Neuman on the cover. He comes out of Ravenwood with the *MAD* book under his arm. I did not expect that. I have no idea why he wanted it, but I wasn't going to question Mr. Irons. We went right on the Internet and had it by next-day air."

"Macon is, by nature, a Dark Caster who has chosen to be a Light Caster because [he wants] to protect Lena, his niece," Kurland explained. "There's a certain formality to Macon, but also a certain pompousness. There is a wit and quickness to him. Although he cannot be his true nature, to a certain degree he shows he still embraces the Dark in the way he dresses. His looks evolve throughout the piece to whatever the scene is and the moment he happens to be in, because he can be anything he wants to be at any time. That's his power, that's part of his joy. For me, it was great because he had a great deal of variety; you could go different places with him. There's a town-hall meeting at the church where Mrs. Lincoln is giving a fire-and-brimstone speech about Lena, and he comes in to interrupt the meeting, looking very much the elegant Southern

"Ravenwood was a one-shot deal, the house where the director said we could do whatever we want. So I came up with this wild idea for the dining room, where the dinner party happens, this amazing glass room that *moves.*"

—Richard Sherman,
production designer

" I adored Ravenwood Manor. I was surprised that the [exterior location house] had as much darkness and mystery as the fictional one. "

—**Alice Englert,** actor

gentleman, very dapper in a dark blue suit with a vest. But at Lena's Claiming, he's very formal in a dark gray suit with a very high collar."

Macon's supernatural power is manifest in his home. Although Ravenwood's exterior never changes, beyond its doors is another world, a space that changes to fit his mood and desires. At one point, LaGravenese asked his production designer how they should describe Ravenwood. "I said, 'It's kind of like Macon's whim,'" Sherman recalled. "Whenever he wakes up in the morning, his first thought is, 'Where shall I live today?' And the house becomes that. The house is kind of a character on its own."

"I WANT YOU TO DO WHATEVER YOU WANT. YOUR WILDEST DREAM."

Sherman, Flemming, and Sizemore initially designed an interior that was a contrast to the drab and decaying exterior but that fit its architectural style—a big stairway with rooms off to each side, and period details. "Richard looked at it and said, 'This is great,'" Sherman recalled. "Then he put the drawing away, turned to me, and said, 'Okay, as pretty as this is, I want you to do whatever you want. Your wildest dream.' So

" I was attracted to Macon because of his mysterious and enigmatic character, which is always fun to play. In this instance, the setting is also central to the story, and Macon is a man of his place, the South. "

—**Jeremy Irons,** actor

we did. It's a different take on a house."

"In the book, it almost seems like the house is alive and connected with Macon—it interacts with him and changes at his will, so every time you see it, it's different," Flemming added. "So Richard [Sherman] and Richard the director wanted to keep that going but make it a little more subtle. The house exterior and interior are so different. It's a surprise when you walk through that door."

"The director said when you open the front door, it shouldn't be what you expect, because these people can make their environment whatever they want it to be," Sizemore added. "That was a complete flip for us. It was very liberating, but also challenging. What could it be when we open the door, what's going to happen, what's the surprise inside this house? What we made is a physical set, but not so abstract that you feel like you jump-cut to another world. And having Jeremy Irons playing the guy who lives there, very sophisticated and holding a

(above) Eileen Atkins, Alice Englert, and Margo Martindale on the Ravenwood set.

The dining room set was constructed on top of a complex apparatus to allow it to move in different directions.

MAD magazine, kind of sells it."

"The interior of Ravenwood sort of looks like the inside of the Guggenheim Museum," the director said, laughing. "It's this gorgeous, enormous room with a freestanding corkscrew-shaped staircase in the center, a giant fireplace, and amazing black furniture. The house is clearly a giant rectangle, but the interior is more circular."

One of the beautiful spaces at Ravenwood is Lena's room. "She has just moved into Ravenwood, and Macon probably made the room beautiful for her, but it still has an old-world plantation home feel to it," Flemming said. "It has this darker wallpaper, purple-black and goldlike tones. It's very cozy and feminine, a little bit eclectic and antique-y, a really beautiful room. We also threw in some more modern elements, like posters of current-day artists and a record collection."

A centerpiece of Ravenwood is its sumptuous dining room, which provides a pivotal sequence for a family dinner with Macon, Lena, Aunt Del, and Gramma. Crashing the party is Ridley, who has brought Ethan along, against his will. Ridley became a Dark Caster on her own sixteenth birthday, and she's a trickster and a temptress—the girl can't help it. "We first see Ridley in a sexy brown-auburn brush-cut hairstyle, very flip and frivolous, with a scarf over her head, driving a convertible—recklessly—down the road," said Terry Baliel.

"Emmy was so fantastic," added Jeffrey Kurland. "She is outlandish, but there's a certain elegance and sexiness to her. She pulls from the past and present for her looks. We had a lot of fun with her. She's very individual; no one else looks like her. She wore very little adornment, maybe a ring or bracelet. It was mostly in her clothes and her body. Her hair changed a lot, and we show a lot of leg."

When Ridley makes trouble at the family dinner, she gets more than she bargained for as Lena stirs up a hurricane—indoors. The elemental fury causes the room to start vibrating, shaking, and then spinning. The effect would be created for real, with visual effects adding the CG storm and other elements. "We did a lot of things practical that most films would have done against green screen," producer Smith explained. "It was very important to Richard to do things for real as much as possible for this entire film. We wanted that sense that everything could happen in real life. Lena's powers were all the elements of nature, so this made it really fun to try and do things practical."

Producer Stoff agreed. "I've made a lot of big effects movies, and my experience is to shoot practical as much as possible. Whatever you can accomplish in camera is always going to look way better. And then you can enhance it digitally."

"We worked closely with special effects," art director Flemming said. "We knew [that] the room was going to do a lot of stuff, that they were going to build a big gimbal rig for that set. The design evolved from the idea that things are not what they seem. Then it was about it being a glass room." Gimbals are pivoted supports that allow the set to be shifted or rotated.

That final inspiration was the Grand Palais ("Grand Palace") in Paris, built in 1900 for an international exhibition.

" The table with Jeremy Irons and Margo Martindale was spinning one way; Emmy Rossum and Alice Englert were spinning counterclockwise—I think they took particular pride in doing it in camera. It was just a different starting point, and more organic, but that's what's going to make that scene different and fun. We were joking with Richard: 'That *effect* was so great!' 'No, *we shot it that way*!' It was one of the most interesting sets I've ever walked on. It was an extremely difficult thing, but Rich and the actors are to be commended. It was a cool thing to watch. "

—**David Moritz**, film editor

Margo Martindale as Aunt Del.

“I had such a wonderful cast. And it was an honor to work with Margo Martindale and Eileen Atkins, two of the best stage actresses around. I couldn’t have lucked out better with the cast.”

—**Richard LaGravenese**, director

Such international showcases often inspired architects to design and build dramatic structures, but the Grand Palais became a permanent landmark of the Paris skyline (as did the Eiffel Tower, built for an 1889 exhibition). Covering an estimated 775,000 square feet, with a glass roof said to be the biggest in Europe, the Palais has the look of a gigantic Victorian greenhouse.[5] That aesthetic was applied to the space of Ravenwood’s dining room, with glass walls, art nouveau flourishes, and crystal chandeliers. The dining room set was also connected to the main Ravenwood interior set via a section of hallway that could be removed when the room needed to spin. The final set was made of steel to withstand the punishment it would take, courtesy of the special effects department.

Alice Englert with Eileen Atkins as Gramma.

Matt Kutcher says he never would have attempted the “spinning-room effect” if he didn’t have the confidence his department could do it. “I’ve built motion bases and turntables for people, cars, and jets. I’ve made things that can turn three hundred sixty degrees or go upside down or backward. But this particular room needed to have six axes of motion—up, down, left, right, front, and back. It also needed to vibrate with the wind; the center of the room needed to spin [in] one direction, and the dining room table needed to spin in the other! And if that wasn’t complicated enough,

Cast and crew on set for the big dinner scene.

the warehouse we were shooting in gave us only so many feet of clearance, and I couldn't dig down to put in a motion base."

The set was more than sixty feet long and about two stories tall, by Kutcher's estimates. The problem was they weren't shooting in a movie soundstage with high ceilings and grids but in a converted warehouse where they were at the max in terms of ceiling clearance. Since they didn't have room for the normal motion-base hydraulics, Kutcher and his crew designed the base on short air bags, as they had done for *Snakes on a Plane* (2006), with two opposite spinning turntables for the floor and the dining room table. Originally, the air-bag system was adapted to handle a glass set where the most "violent" motion would go through a "dampener," as Kutcher called it, to take the shake out so the glass wouldn't shatter. But at the last moment, the glass was replaced with Plexiglas. "At the last minute, we decided that with all the shaking the room was going to do, that Plexiglas would be lighter and more

Emmy Rossum as Lena's cousin Ridley Duchannes.

“It’s amazing how swiftly technology progresses. The downside is [that] even the best visual effect of only a year ago gets outdated. But we attempted to shoot as much of our ‘magic’ in camera as possible. It was an artistic decision I thoroughly enjoyed. On the other hand, I think the spinning room helped us more with a headache than anything.”

—**Alice Englert,** actor

flexible,” Flemming explained. “We normally don’t like to use Plexiglas in place of glass because it never looks as good and there [are] often distortions in the reflections. But in this case, we were heavily aging the glass, so that ended up not being a problem.”

The special effects crew would be able to move the set with inches of ceiling space to spare. Kutcher likened it to the mast of a sailboat at sea—if a swell caused the front of the ship to dip, everything moved, including the mast, which would rise proportionately higher into the air. “We could drop one side of the set from zero to thirty inches. We had to move and articulate it within inches, not only for people’s safety, but so that it didn’t spin the set into the ceiling.”

For operational control, Kutcher decided not to use a computer-controlled motion system but to be, literally, hands on. “We actually backed out of the technicality of it and put everything in good old hand controllers, like they used to run in amusement parks. So we would hold valves for each one to spin and move, basically. Although it was new technology, we operated it old school.”

Kutcher had a control station outside the dining room set with a sight line inside when the doors were open. When the doors had to be closed, “witness cameras”—essentially a camera feed to the monitors—provided complete views inside the set. One operator moved the

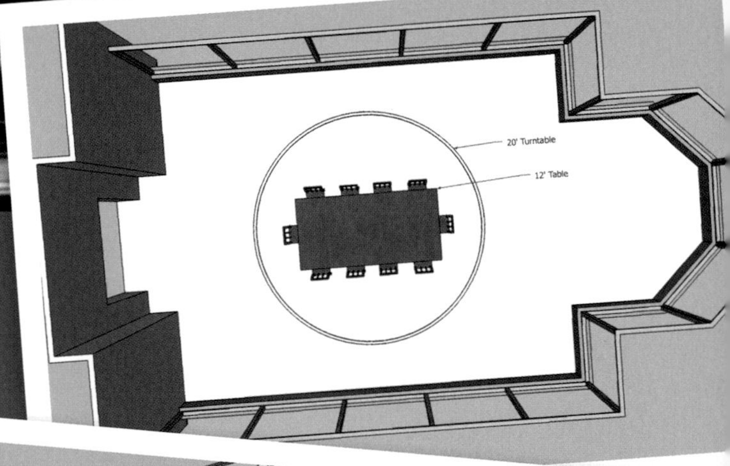

The complex designs for the gimbal mechanism and the actual gear assembly placed underneath the dining room set to rotate and tilt the room.

Designs and photos courtesy Spectrum FX

❝ I was born in March of 1961, and that very day my dad quit a construction job in New York City. Three months later he went to LA and became a stand-in for his brother Paul, who was playing second lead on *The Untouchables* TV show. I pretty much grew up in the business. My dad worked on the old *Batman* TV series, doing a lot of stunt fights and parts on the show. I was five years old and got to visit the *Batman* set and see the Batcave. I remember sliding down the Batpole. That was my first introduction to the stunt world. ❞

—Chuck Picerni Jr.,
stunt coordinator

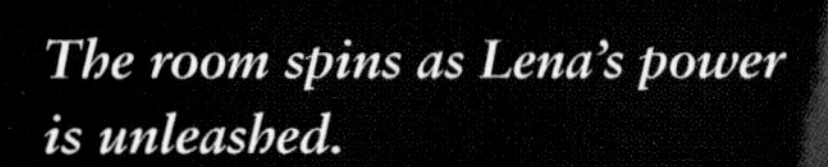

The room spins as Lena's power is unleashed.

air bags of the motion base, another operator controlled the spinning of the floor and the table, and a third made the chandelier spin, while four operators worked the wind machines.

Every element had been choreographed in Kutcher's early discussions with the director, who planned everything down to such fine details as how each actor at the table would react when vibration plates begin shaking glasses of water (as in *Jurassic Park* when approaching dinosaurs cause a glass of water to quake). "As the chandelier would start to rock in a specific way, everything would accelerate," Kutcher explained. "The table would begin to spin, and the floor would spin in the opposite direction. The entire set moved on multiple axes, and the wind machines increased at speeds upward of sixty miles per hour. The twelve-foot dining room table spun once every three seconds—with all the witches, older and younger, at the table. The chandelier was an air ram that moved it from side to side, but an electric motor spun it three hundred sixty degrees. It was a lot of elements."

Troy Sizemore likened the final steel set to a gigantic metal birdcage. "Normal scenery would fall apart under such stress, but this set kind of lent itself to the shaking because a metal cage is very strong. What special effects did is build a deck, with a gimbal under the deck. It was quite a complicated mechanism. When they finished the deck, we put on the set. And it rode like a mechanical bull, essentially."

The set was completely tested before two grueling days of filming. There was also the chance to "ride" the room before they'd shoot it for real. "That was a freaking expensive set!" exclaimed Joe Harkins. "The first time we went in for a demo was sort of scary. I was getting seasick and had to leave. Five minutes was a good enough demo for me! It was like an insane amusement-park ride. You're seeing reflections from the walls, and the whole room could go up and down and move. Then the floor spun in one direction, the table spun the other."

During their face-off, Lena literally blows Ridley out of the room, an in-camera effect produced by the stunt department. "Matt Kutcher did a phenomenal job building the room and the spinning," said stunt coordinator Chuck Picerni. "He and I worked hand in hand to coordinate my action with the people involved. We had prep time and went over what the director wanted to see, how we were going to go about it, how the table was going to spin. Then I put my rigging in to complement that.

"I had a stunt double for Emmy Rossum, and we ratcheted her out on wires," Picerni continued. "It's a combination of things working together to get a body to fly. The ratchet is basically a pneumatic ram that's calculated by air pressure. We set it to a certain level that determines not only the speed with which she comes out but the height and distance she travels. Depending on a particular sequence, the actor or stunt double wears what we call a hanging harness or a jerk vest—in this case, it was the jerk vest. We find a pick point on the vest for the level we want to fly her at, and attach it with a shackle. You have pick points in the ceiling that come down to her, [and the wire], in turn, goes to the ratchet. On a stunt like this—and depending on the budget of the show—you sometimes try to hide the wires. We didn't have to worry about that, because they had CGI digital imagery to do [and would digitally erase the wires]."

The dinner party required the prop department to get safety dishes and glasses that wouldn't break when the spinning started, and hire a food stylist and caterer to not only provide a

Kyle Gallner as Ridley's brother, Larkin.

feast—lobster tail and pheasant, mashed potatoes, and corn and peas were on the menu—but also clean up and reset the meal between takes. "The actors were actually eating before the table started to spin—one of the actors continued to eat while the table was spinning!" Yeaton said. "It all had to be functional food, and we brought in two huge refrigerators to keep things fresh and cook on the spot, and we had to keep going to the grocery store for this and that. It was one of those things that will look seamless, but you'll never know the pain we had! The director and I hugged each other when they called 'Wrap' at the end of those two days! It was such a relief."

"Oh, it was so emotional watching these people spin like that," Kutcher exclaimed. "Some of [the actors] were younger, some were older, but they all looked pretty green. Oh my God, what a thing to do to human beings! To spin someone in one direction and some in the other direction, and then, just as they were able to sustain the spinning, we'd move the floor right out from under their feet. I don't know how they even remembered their lines. I don't know if they didn't just want to scream to get off! What a wild Mr. Toad ride. No one wanted to cry wolf, to be the first one to say 'Get me out of here!' But every time it stopped, they all looked pretty relieved. They were unbelievable troupers, each and every one."

Joe Harkins had his own concerns about the spinning room. In postproduction, he had to add the indoor storm, CG objects flying off the table, and ether, the by-product of the supernatural energy. "The room is spinning, and you have to figure out how to shoot all this stuff and track the shot so you can put in all this visual effects stuff," Harkins explained. "When there's nothing to lock onto in the environment, it's hard to make things work perfectly in CG. Your plate

"The [spinning dining room] was a phenomenal amount of beautiful complications."

—**Matt Kutcher**, special effects supervisor

"[Ravenwood] is about beautiful gardens and an incredible house. Since Macon has so little to fill his time, we decided he would enjoy using what supernatural powers he had to modernize the interior in a way that would surprise a visitor who had only seen the house from the outside."

—**Jeremy Irons**, actor

The command center for operating the dining room set.

is sort of blurry with all this stuff going on, and you have to add the CG on top of that. Finally we were like, 'Screw it, just shoot it, and we'll figure it out.' It was a little more work with the integration of what was already there, as opposed to just having shot on green screen and you can do whatever you want. The general idea with visual effects is you start with the least amount of information you need in the plate, then add what you need. With green screen you have more options. Now, no matter what I do, I've got a spinning room."

Although there would be a couple of green-screen shots in the sequence, the director had no regrets about going with a physical effect. "You had to be there on the Saturday when I brought in the cast to see it and ride it before we had to shoot it," LaGravenese said. "They were so excited because, I guess, they usually are in front of green screen, where they're not really interacting with anything. I could have done it on green screen, but my feeling is an audience can subconsciously tell the difference. The spinning table and spinning floor and the shaking room are all happening, and that affected the performances. And Eileen Atkins was really nauseous! [*laughs*] I felt so bad! I had to take Dramamine to direct it, because I have terrible motion sickness. Jeremy said, 'But you weren't on the table.' I said, 'I know, but I had to *watch* it!'"

"In our film, that idea is [the visual effects] sort of sneak up on you," David Moritz added. "You want to make sure that when the room starts spinning, it's been created by this conflict with Ridley. Lena has power over the elements; her emotions can trigger wind and storms and lightning, so it comes from that. The fun of the scene is it's two teenagers behaving very badly at a family dinner! But they are also supernatural beings, and when they get pissed off, it's a whole different thing—they create a tornado. The humor of that is not lost on me."

CHAPTER 4

“The walls of this round room are covered in a kind of prehistoric fresco paint job, and these paintings are threatening to the human. They are the guardians, and they don’t want [Ethan] there. *You shouldn’t be down here.*”

—**Troy Sizemore**, supervising art director

Months after production wrapped, Emma Thompson reflected on *Beautiful Creatures*: "The world of the film was wonderfully mysterious—full of sinister beauty and the sense of otherworldly beings in close proximity, felt but never quite seen."

The character of Amma was a mortal who embodied that sensibility. She had also metamorphosed; she had always been a seer, but now she held the keys to the magical Caster Library.

Early in the production, LaGravenese and Kurland had discussed how best to reflect Amma's African roots and spirituality. "She has a certain amount of [flowing] garments, but it's to keep with the contemporary nature of who she is," Kurland explained. "Amma is living in this town and runs the library, so there's a certain intellectual quality to her. But you also see evidence of a spiritual past in the way she dresses and the jewelry she wears. I used a good deal of chiffon and fabrics that move and flow. And she also wears a lot of copper and handmade jewelry reminiscent of African ceremonial jewelry; her rings and such all bring forward a spiritual past. I didn't want

Ethan (Alden Ehrenreich) and Amma (Viola Davis).

Sketches courtesy Jeffrey Kurland

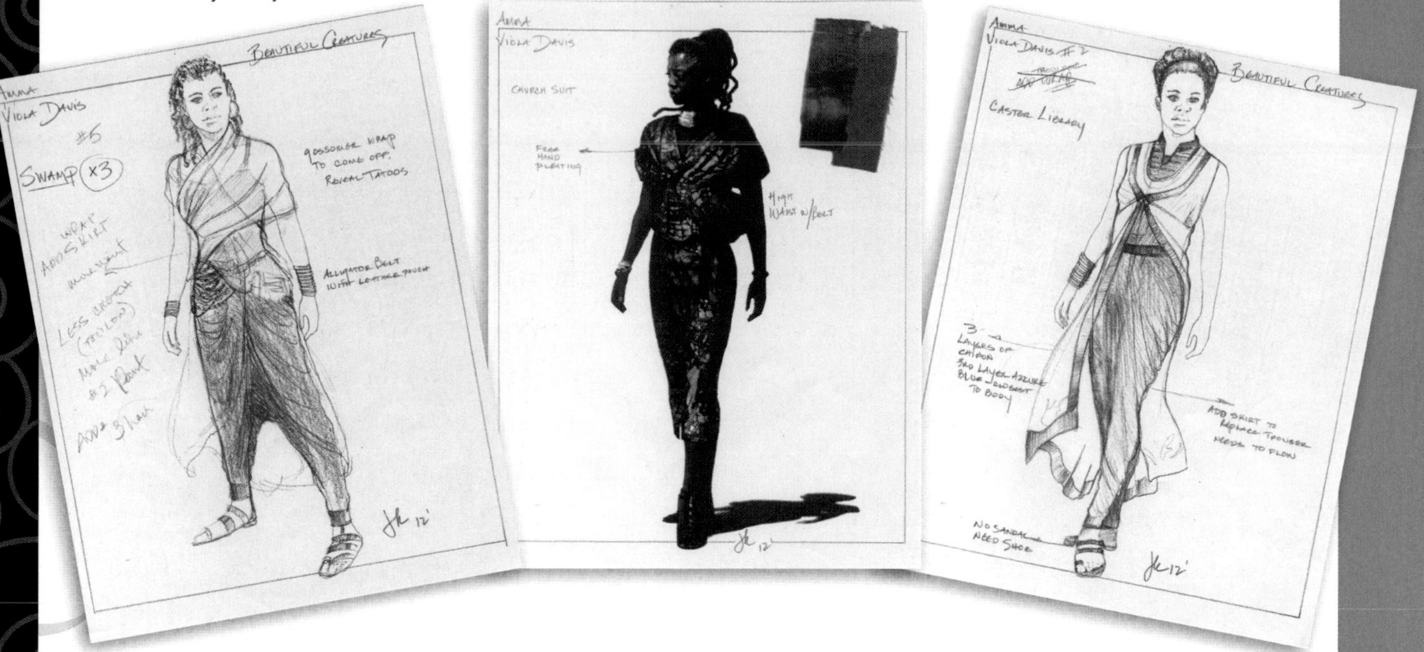

Costume sketches for Amma.

to hit you over the head. It isn't directly adapted from actual African patterns, but you see a hint of it. It's still contemporary and American, but all very individual to her."

"When I went into the costume fitting," Viola Davis recalled, "I liked the direction he was going in. I liked how all the costumes I wore flowed and had a lightness—even when she walks, it just kind of billows in the wind. And the alligator belt he had me wear, and the jewelry! The costume—absolutely; but the accessories—fantastic, really, really fantastic. I understood who she was in the contemporary world, and I understood the connections she had with the past."

During Kurland's research into African culture, he also noticed the tradition of scarification and keloid tattooing. Viola Davis recalls that when the costume designer first came to her house to discuss her character, he brought along inspirational photographs that included African women with tribal scarification. "Jeffrey had a photograph of this woman who had tribal scars from her ankles to, literally, the top of her head. They had images of women with different headdresses, the braids, which I thought was too extreme. I didn't want any big red flags that people would know *this* is the woman who was going to be the channeler, the seer. I just didn't want my character to take people out of the movie. I wanted them to be able to go into this fictitious small town and not think, *What is* she *doing there?* I didn't want it to look like I was voodoo woman, like she'd walk into the grocery store and fall to the ground, foaming at the mouth and channeling spirits. I wanted her to look a little different, eccentric, but still be part of the community. And I think Jeffrey did a great job with that."

Gatlin was like any small town,

Amma (Viola Davis) speaks with her ancestors.

Amma, as mortal and seer, is a bridge between the physical reality of sleepy Gatlin and the hidden world of the Casters. Amma's spiritual and supernatural side was a key part of her personality in the novel, where she was imagined with ancestry rooted in the Gullah people, many of whom trace their heritage back to slaves who had been brought to South Carolina. "A lot of them were healers," Kami Garcia explained. "That seemed the perfect model for Amma's spirituality, that she would have roots in Gullah culture and these powerful women. Even though we go back in time to slavery and the Civil War, we wanted to show this power that so many people who were enslaved brought with them and were able to maintain, even though white society didn't recognize it. Even if they were just a cook in someone's house, they had this whole other thing."

But Viola Davis wanted Amma to belong to the Yoruba, a people of West Africa who are primarily located in Nigeria. "The thing about *Beautiful Creatures* that I absolutely love is that in a genre like this, they'll usually go forward in time, but this one goes *back*

noted Davis, who grew up in the small city of Central Falls, Rhode Island. It was the kind of place where you saw familiar faces from childhood to adulthood, where you would probably marry your childhood sweetheart, where everyone attended the same church—a place that never seemed to change. "But it's got a secret side to it," Davis added. "All of a sudden, as the characters are peeled away, you see this history and this energy that is absolutely otherworldly, that makes it unlike any town you've ever seen."

> "I'm in the business of truth telling."
>
> —**Viola Davis**, actor

in time! And I just made the decision, as an actor, that I wanted to go back further [with Amma's spirituality]. The Gullah did not intrigue me as much as the Yoruba background, which is older and was the whole basis for voodoo, and even has some basis in Roman Catholic faith, and has different goddesses."

In the film, as in the book, Amma goes to a cemetery in the swamp to ask for the intercession of ancestral spirits. For the scene, Davis recalled a visit she made to Gambia in 1991, when she was twenty-five years old. There she met a griot, and that was the figure she conjured in her mind as Amma invoked the other world and prayed in the Yoruba tongue.

"The griots are the oldest member of a tribe, and they carry the history. I just had this image of her channeling this griot who was coming back and giving some word of wisdom. In my head, I had the image of the griot I met in Africa when I was twenty-five years old."

During the cemetery scene, Amma's scarification is revealed. Makeup department head Fionagh Cush had previously worked out a scarification design, but when the character's ancestral roots changed to Yoruba, Cush had to change the look. "I had to do a lot of research on Yoruba scarification, and thank God for the Internet, because we were stuck on location three hours outside New Orleans. I had to make sure any design I picked didn't mean anything bad or derogatory.... We came up with our own. It's not a literal translation but influenced by [the African] artwork."

Macon (Jeremy Irons) and Amma (Viola Davis) have a past connection.

Cush sculpted the scar designs on a flat surface, with smaller silicone molds poured up for sections that broke down the sculpted designs, allowing for mixing and matching various sections. "These silicone molds are thin, flexible, and fairly clear, so you can see exactly where they are being placed on the skin," Cush said. "After mixing up thickened Pros-Aide [a commercial prosthetic adhesive] to the correct skin tone, along with CAB-O-SIL, which is used to thicken liquids and certain food products, [the mixure] is put into the molds and allowed to dry. A little more Pros-Aide can then be applied to the underside of the scars while still in the molds, to ensure good adhesion. Once a position on the body has been decided, you simply press the loaded mold onto the skin. This mold is then peeled away, leaving the scar on the skin, which is then sealed."

The Caster Library represents mystical knowledge and magic manifesting through time and space. The production design took its cue from the novel, which described columns from different civilizations lining the main library's endless hallways. "That set evolved very slowly over the course of our prep," Flemming explained. "Our talented sculptor, Brent

Building the entrace to the Caster Library.

The intricate set for the Caster Library; (insets) Lena reads **The Book of Moons**, *and one of the sculpted columns.*

Barnidge, did a lot of sculptures for this set and designed... bas-reliefs and stuff from different cultures. I gathered reference material from different temples and different cultures. We also brought in iconography that was magic-related, from witchcraft and Wiccan and Druid [traditions]. A lot of those references are very elemental—water, wind, earth—and we used those symbols in the many carvings by Brent for columns designed by Richard and myself."

Before construction coordinator Randy Coe was given the blueprints, the art department did schematic drawings to make sure the library would fit the stage. A scale cardboard model, complete with little human figures, was built so that the director and producers could better understand the space. "It's fun to go on a computer screen and do a walk-through of a virtual three-D environment because it's dazzling and people get all heated up," Troy Sizemore said. "But with a paper model, everybody can understand it and sign off on it, especially when you're budgeting. If they say they need to reduce the cost, well, you just take a knife and cut a part of the model off. That's the back-and-forth before the drawings are done. You have to make sure you have the right size for

> “The Caster Library was not supposed to be eerie; it was supposed to be magical. That was the key.”
>
> **—Richard Sherman,** production designer

the budget and the scene.

"You can do the drawings pretty quickly after that, and start laying it out on the stage. This set had a lot of plaster that was cast. It was supposed to be ancient, and you get that texture from plaster you can't get from a sleeker, cleaner surface. The columns were sixteen feet because, with the format of the film, everything is letterboxed and down low. You detail to camera; you don't want to build them twenty-five feet and waste a lot of money up in the air. Money is eye level."

The set built on the warehouse stage would be one hundred forty feet long, starting from what Sizemore estimated as a platform height of twenty-eight feet, then descending down stairs to a round room that was thirty feet in diameter. "The set itself was a series of four spaces that had to start way up in the air," Sizemore explained. "The idea was that you could shoot it continuously, and it all felt very real for the actors and every-one else because it was one continuous

The production design included nods to many ancient civilizations, such as these Hindu-inspired doors.

physical space. The first space appeared to be a basement of the town library, so it was what you would expect in a basement, with ducting, storage, and a greasy old boiler."

The round room—what Lorin Flemming called "the Stair Room"—was designed as "the most ancient of spaces," she explained. "Richard, our director, really wanted to get across that these witches have been around, and among us, through time and history. He wanted this space in particular to convey that. As you go down into the round room, with tunnels that branch off in every direction, it was more weathered and ancient. This was our ancient entryway."

Ethan and Lena visit the secret library, with Amma leading the way. She first takes the key from around her neck and opens the basement door. Viola Davis described the effect as opening onto the mythical realm of Shangri-La.

"It's these steps that lead [in] different directions and go through archways representing different entryways into worlds," she said. "And underneath the staircase is this water, like living water. And you walk down these stairs, and you walk into this most extraordinary library, with a high ceiling and beams

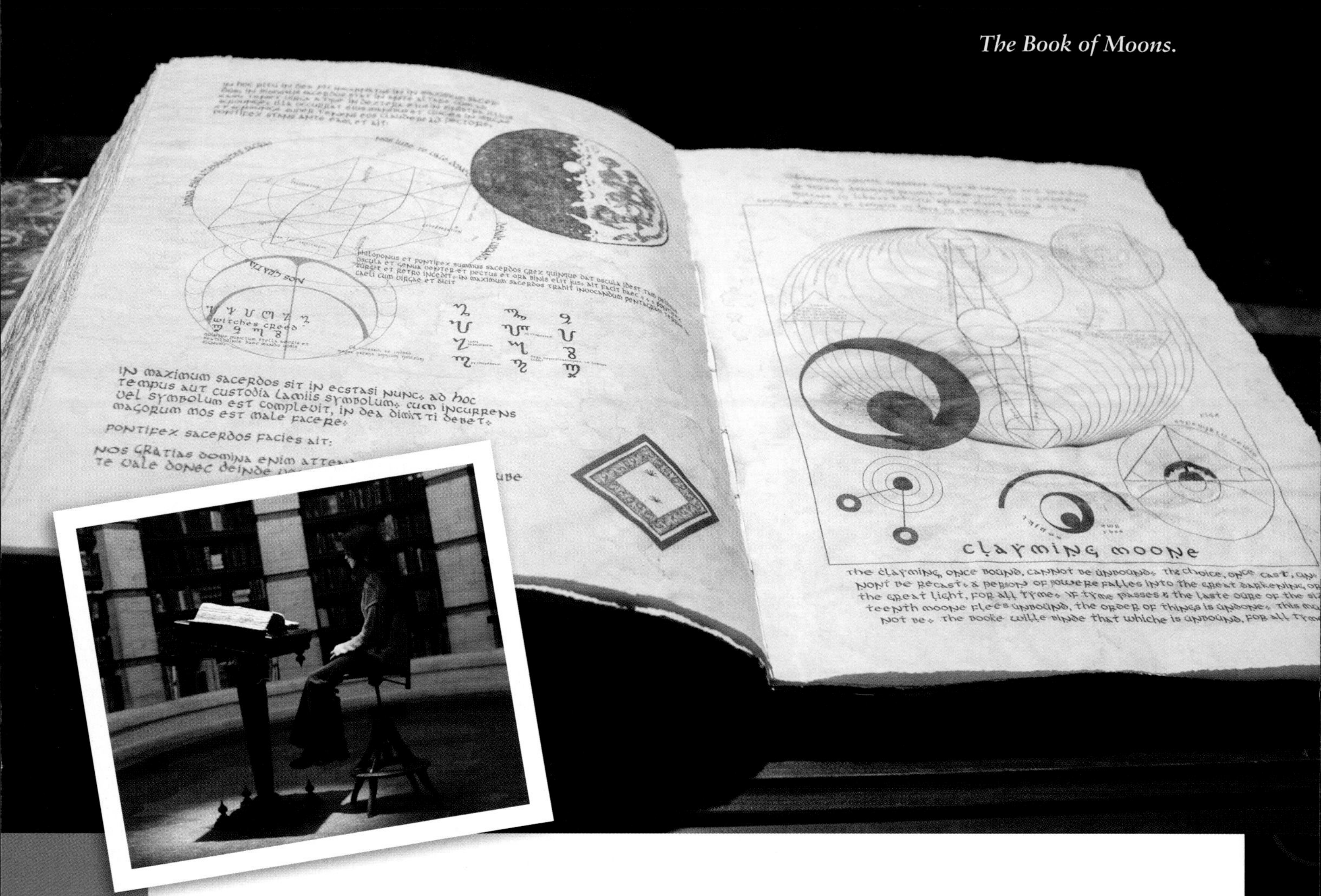

The Book of Moons.

and sculptures from Africa and Europe. And then you walk farther through these doors and you have this whole other sanctuary where you have the sacred book that has the answers and every spell that's ever existed. . . . The only way I can describe it is it's a great mixture of the mortal world and the otherworld."

"Portraying these different civilizations was fun to do," Sherman said. "We designed and built massive columns that were Egyptian and Etruscan and Roman. We had fake bronze doors that might have something Hindu on them, [and] the flooring would be all Aztec. It's a huge room lined with books and massive columns that we made, with six big study tables and chairs that sort of look like they're growing out of the floor, with crescent moon tops made of copper. This big room has stacks and hallways and tunnels, and we have green screen behind all of that."

"The tunnels in the library will lead off into infinity, so we had green screen in there, and we extend it in CG," added visual effects supervisor Harkins. "The production design and art department did fantastic work that we basically added to, while adhering to Richard LaGravenese's vision. We were trying to make magic in there that didn't look like Hogwarts [from *Harry Potter*], or anything like that. The mission was to be subtle, to have it be integrated and look real, and not be over the top or in your face."

> "It's hard when you have the idea that the library is one of the most magical places in the story—what do you do with that?"
>
> **—Lorin Flemming,** art director

At one end of this main library was the room with the sacred book Davis noted, an inner sanctum known as the Sanctuary, the repository for *The Book of Moons*. The Sanctuary was an oval room designed with some of the same carved elements as those in the main library space, but existing only to hold the formidable book that sat on a podium carved with Gothic elements and witchcraft-influenced moon phase symbols. "The book has a presence, a life of its own," said Flemming, who designed it.

To bring the book's design to life, Brook Yeaton worked with the Hand Prop Room. The result, some eighteen inches long, twelve inches wide, and six inches thick, had the look of a family Bible from the eighteen hundreds, with brass hardware to seal and lock its leather cover. "It's a very spooky-looking book, for lack of a better [term]," Yeaton said.

Viola Davis, Alice Englert, and Alden Ehrenreich shoot a scene that will later have special effects added to it.

Lena (Alice Englert) and Amma (Viola Davis).

"They bound it with thread, the way it would have been done in the eighteen hundreds. We did a couple of pages of writing, just to have something for the actors to react to."

The visual effects department would enhance the Caster Library. "We added a glowing pool of water to the entryway, as well as animated sculptures that react to Ethan and Lena's presence in the main library," Joe Harkins said. "We also provided a breathing effect for *The Book of Moons*, with magic coming off it, and writing appearing inside."

"It was so great to be on a film where each department was really at the top of their game," Ehrenreich said. "Being in a movie where the crew was as talented as it was brought the film up to a different level. I felt buoyed by the talent all around me, cast and crew."

The Caster Library was another example of the production aesthetic of making fantasy real. For Viola Davis, the physical set was as magical as its premise. "It was just unbelievable, like the greatest library you've ever seen but with this whole other element—it's also the gateway [between worlds]. I felt, as an actor walking through it, that the set was a character in and of itself. It was living and breathing, and I was basically the gatekeeper. The designers did a wonderful job with that, and I'm sure the CGI effects will heighten it.

"I would rather have a set instead of a green screen. I have no problem using my imagination, but sometimes you can

“THE SET WAS A CHARACTER IN AND OF ITSELF. IT WAS LIVING AND BREATHING, AND I WAS BASICALLY THE GATEKEEPER.”

take that to the limit. What people don’t understand is, it’s hard for an actor to act in a vacuum. Every actor, every prop, the set itself, is part of the collaboration. That being said, you look at people like Harrison Ford who really do it well, and you think, *Oh my God, I give it up to you. You can make me believe that you are actually in this world, and you’re acting to this green screen.* But I would much rather see a set.”

Davis played most of her scenes with Jeremy Irons, Alden Ehrenreich, and Alice Englert, and she applauded the skill and professionalism they brought to their characters and the work. “What was great was they all had a process, a way to work in order to create a character and get to the truth of a scene. They weren’t just winging it. Some people don’t have a process. I appreciated the fact that they all did. And Alden and Alice were such mature, highly intelligent young actors. They came with a wisdom; they came with a fearlessness.

“I went to school with actors who would fling themselves against walls and do weird things. I have sat in audiences watching actors like that and thinking, *I don’t know who they are.* When I saw *The Lord of the Rings*, as fantastical as it was, I believed it. You believe these actors are who they say they are, that they live and breathe in this very specific world. That has to come from a place that’s grounded and specific and real that you’ve created, not something you kind of put on. Acting is not putting on. Acting is embodying.”

Ethan (Alden Ehrenreich) and Amma (Viola Davis).

CHAPTER 5

The Caster Ball

“Jeffrey wanted *everything*. The story line went that these people were bored and dressed for their own amusement. It wasn’t just about high fashion, but high fashion with an odd twist to it. We bounced ideas back and forth until the very day [we shot the sequence], and tweaked things on the day.”

—**Terry Baliel**, hair department head

The painting shows a man wearing a bowler hat and dressed in a buttoned gray overcoat and a red tie, standing in front of a low gray wall. Look closer and you see one of the three coat buttons is either missing or hidden. The strangest thing is there's a green apple, suspended in the air, hiding the man's face. Welcome to René Magritte's *Le fils de l'homme* ("The Son of Man"), a painting that gives a snapshot of surrealism, a movement by artists who believed that dreams were more real than reality.

The Blank Check, a Magritte painting of a strange forest where a horse and rider appear to be dissected into sections against the trees, provided inspiration for LaGravenese and cinematographer Philippe Rousselot when they designed a scene where Macon catches Ethan in a binding spell—they dubbed it "the Magritte run." But the surrealists would really shine at the party thrown for Lena's Claiming, what some of the team called "the Caster Ball."

The gathering of Casters was one of the inspirations that came to the director during filming. The costume designer, who took the lead in developing the sequence, estimated the idea popped up in mid-March 2012. It was shot in mid-May, toward the end of principal photography. "It was never talked about," makeup head Cush noted. "It wasn't in the script. Then all of a sudden it was, 'We're doing *what* outside? This will be interesting!'"

LaGravenese recalls it began when he and Rousselot were on a location scout, puzzling over how to stage Lena's Claiming. In the novel, the scene was presented as a ritualistic ceremony, with Lena in the center of a circle of Casters

Macon (Jeremy Irons), Lena (Alice Englert), and Gramma (Eileen Atkins) at the ball.

The intricate and surreal Caster Ball scene.

chanting mysterious Latin verses. "I didn't know how I would shoot it, and I was just feeling frustrated that day. Film makes everything literal, so what works in a novel in relationship with your own imagination won't necessarily translate to a literal creation of it, when you have real people and locations and someone else's imagination telling you how it looks. And everyone knew and supported my goal that nothing look like something we've seen, and we've seen movies where people are standing in a circle chanting in Latin.

"So then we decided it would be like a Sweet Sixteen coming-out party for a witch. A lot of Casters have to be there and don't want to be and are kind of bored. I told [Jeffrey Kurland] I wanted a combination of the "Ascot Gavotte" [scene from *My Fair Lady*] and [fashion designer] Alexander McQueen. Each character was to come from some organic, supernaturally elemental power. We had a garden set design [for the Claiming], and I had to throw that out when I had this new idea. What Richard, Lorin, and Troy came up with was amazing. And Jeffrey and his people came up with twenty-five insanely original Caster costumes. *This* felt original, and everyone helped create it."

"Richard LaGravenese decided it would be more of a surreal celebration," Flemming recalled. "We ended up doing a mosaic, a checkerboard patio with giant gold and black and silver reflective orbs, some of them as big as four feet in diameter. They were made in China [and] got banged up during shipping, and there was no time to get new ones shipped. But our prop makers came up with a great idea—they forced compressed air into them and popped out all the dents. [The final result] was almost like a sculpture garden. The greens department created this garden with about forty giant, sixteen-foot cypress trees to surround it. The orbs reflected the black-and-white checkerboard patterns and the people in these amazing, surrealist costumes—the set itself had an M. C. Escher–esque feel to it."

The "Ascot Gavotte" sequence from the film *My Fair Lady* was a stylized scene of a high-society day at the races that featured a monochromatic set and wardrobe. That was "the jumping-off point," Kurland said. "We then looked at all the surrealist painters and artists of the twentieth century, pulled in fashion, looked at all sorts of things to create this world of the Casters. I wanted to give a surreal quality to the party, not for them to come off like mortals in fancy clothes. If you look at the world of Magritte and the

A busy wardrobe, makeup, and hair team prepped extras with fanciful Caster costumes.

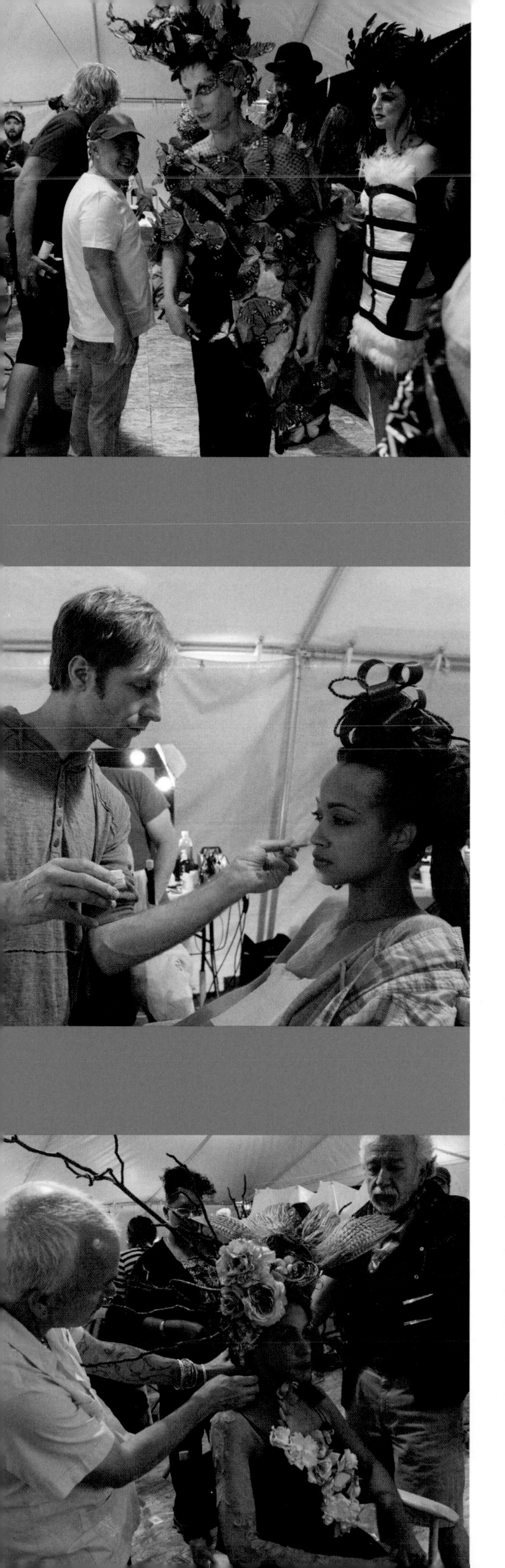

surrealists, an image might look normal, but there's always something slightly off. That was what I was trying to do with the look of that party and what the Casters wore. There's also a lot of nature infused into it, so birds and plants and flowers are all very much a part of their physicality.

"You have the world of Gatlin, but then you have the Casters," Kurland added. "Where do they come from? What makes them unique? The Caster Ball is Lena's coming-out party, but you want to show what their world *is*, that it's not just Lena, Macon, Aunt Del, and Gramma. I think it was Richard's desire to do that, but also to have a certain fun

"I WANTED TO GIVE A SURREAL QUALITY TO THE PARTY."

and playfulness with who they are. Face it—if you had all the power in the world, you would do something with it. You'd have fun with it."

Makeup head Cush observed that fantastical images were always being concocted using computer-generated imagery; why not show what makeup could do? She brought in four artists and painters—two each from Miami and Los Angeles—who would augment the makeup with body-painting effects. Each was assigned a particular Caster, according to their ability, to realize a particular conception in the narrow window of time allowed. "It was such a specialty thing," Cush said. "Every day I was thinking, *What can we do with makeup that's never been seen before?* That was fun and challenging. We were painting people, adding three-dimensional tattoos that would stand off the skin."

The Caster characters included the Cheetah Lady, who wore a skintight leopard-print dress, her hair lacquer-curled on one side of the head with flowers down the other, and face and bare arm airbrush-painted to look like a cheetah. Another Caster was dressed in a starched white coat with a hat and veil, with the hair department twisting black, light, and gray shades of matted hair into knobs on each side of her head and texturing them to look like spiderwebs.

(left) Three intricate costumes; (below) Macon (Jeremy Irons) and Lena (Alice Englert) in their party costumes.

The team invented an amazing array of imaginative looks for the Caster Ball scene.

“With period stuff, you really have to do it by the book, but this party was a total fantasy—we could do whatever we wanted. They’re all witches who have come for the Claiming, and we tried to do something that hadn’t been done before. Wardrobe wanted the makeup to become part of the wardrobe and their makeup to become part of the hair, so they all kind of meld into one.”

—**Fionagh Cush,**
makeup department head

“This was such a fantastic, massive movie for makeup and hair, especially with Jeffrey and Richard being so appreciative and welcoming of anything you could throw at them,” Cush noted. “For example, in the notes from wardrobe, Jeffrey said, ‘I have this suit that’s made of clouds, and I’m just going to put the waistcoat on. Can we paint the rest of his body?’ So we painted his entire body, face, everything, so you can’t see where the wardrobe stops and the body starts; it all melts into one. For Butterfly Lady, we made three-dimensional tattoos so it looked like butterflies were living on her skin. We had one gentleman whose wardrobe was musical notes that I made three-dimensional, using movie hair all over his body and across his face and up the back of his head.”

Meanwhile, wardrobe, makeup, and hair still had to be ready for the work already planned for each day’s filming, while the new sequence, from design to execution, had to be done on the fly. The Caster Ball was also scheduled after the grueling demands of shooting the Civil War–period battle and its reenactment. “We were madly scrambling,” Baliel recalled. “Whenever we had free time for one of us to sneak away from the set and let the other person watch the actors, one of us would go back to the trailer and continue to prep custom wigs and stuff for the party.”

“We were working at an incredible pace just to get it done,” Kurland agreed.

"We all relied on our knowledge. I had a very good crew, we had a great makeup-and-hair crew, and we worked closely together."

Because of the tight schedule, there had been no time for camera tests. "That was the scary thing," Baliel said. "A lot of these looks, especially the makeup, were very specific and intricate. You don't want to make a fool of yourself, of course, so you normally try things out and see what works and what doesn't. But we didn't have any time to do that, so we kind of flew by the seat of our pants that day and made it work."

No idea was too wild for the look of the crowd at the Caster Ball. "They *all* made it in," Fionagh Cush noted. "Richard loved it all and put everything in. He would have shot it for four days if he could and if it wasn't so exhausting for the crew and the people wearing these elaborate outfits. We started at two in the morning, and everyone was ready by eight a.m. for shooting. It took six hours to get these people ready for the ball."

The Southern heat necessitated constant makeup touch-ups on set.

Because the actors were outdoors in the heat and humidity, constant touch-ups were needed. Between takes, umbrellas were held over the partygoers to shield them from the sun. Terry Baliel described the effect the heat had on hair

To have fun with the magical powers of Ridley (Emmy Rossum), the costume designer imagined a range of film-inspired looks for the character.

throughout the filming. "Some of the gals with long hair would go outside and five minutes later their hair would be droopy and limp. A lot of times it'd be clipped up until right before they were ready to roll, and we'd take out the clips and brush their hair. We were out there with butane curling irons trying to keep things fresh and touched up, but there's only so much you can do in a hundred degrees and eighty-five percent humidity. Sometimes hairdos evolved on the set during the day and turned into something a little bit different from what you intended."

The one "cursed" outfit was Antler Lady, Cush reckoned. That Caster character wore antlers on her head, had her face painted green, and wore a green dress designed to look like a deer hiding behind ferns—three girls who wore the outfit all fainted, doubtless because of the heat and heaviness of the headgear.

Another problem for outdoor filming throughout was bugs. "It was so bad with bugs, it was unbelievable," Cush added. "I had to do a lot of research to keep people from being bitten." It wasn't feasible to spray or apply a repellent like DEET, because it would eat away at the makeup. Cush discovered citronella oil, the essence of what is in most bug sprays, that could be topically applied. It was so

Lena (Alice Englert) and her Dark Caster cousin Ridley (Emmy Rossum).

“RIDLEY IS TRYING TO BE A GOOD GIRL WHEN SHE COMES TO THE CASTER PARTY.”

potent that a drop or two did the trick.

Ridley shows up at the ball dressed in a demure outfit that LaGravenese had personally requested, what was the latest in a theme for that character's wardrobe. “Ridley is trying to be a good girl when she comes to the Caster party, so I wanted her to look like Doris Day,” the director explained. “I wanted a pillbox hat and a clutch purse and one of those monochromatic suits Doris Day always wore. And Jeffrey got completely on that, because Jeffrey and I have the same language.

“When I was in prep, I realized I wasn't having enough fun with the magic. I decided that if *I* had supernatural powers, and being a movie geek, I would give myself different identities and play around with looks, just for fun. So I decided to do that with the character of Ridley. I told Jeffrey Kurland that for each of Emmy Rossum's looks, we should do a different iconic female from film. The first look we went for was Louise Brooks, who was an iconic figure and pretty much the bad girl of silent films. In another scene, I wanted her to be the Rita Hayworth character Gilda. There was a scene where Emmy is on a raft with Thomas Mann's character, and I wanted her to look like Marilyn Monroe in *River of No Return*.”

The Caster Ball was judged a success. Although the production hoped to get it all in one day, they were back for a second day in the sun. “It was very, very hot. It was horrendous,” Cush recalled. “But we got through it.”

“I'm never totally satisfied, because I'm always thinking about how I could have made it a little bit better,” Terry Baliel reflected. “Every time I do something, everybody says, ‘Oh my God, that looks great!’ But I'm thinking, *The next time I'll make this part a little higher, or this a little sleeker or darker.*

“But the final effect is always very dramatic. When it begins, you're doing your research, you're looking at clothes on hangers, wigs in the hair-and-makeup trailer, and photos of people in their own hair [and] with no makeup. But when all the different facets come together—when you have people in costumes, with full makeup and hair and headpieces, and you get them on a dramatic set—that's the first time you can take stock of the enormity of what it is you have created.”

CHAPTER 6

Sixteen Moons

“I don’t know why they do [Civil War reenactments]. We were trying to think of any other war, even around the world, that people reenact every weekend. When you look at the Civil War, it was the horror of young people killed and this nation torn apart. It was terrible, and maybe that’s it. Maybe it’s to keep that memory alive, so we don’t forget we have to be united as a nation. That’s what I choose to believe.”

—**Richard LaGravenese**, director

"THE CHALLENGE OF THE MOVIE WAS ALSO THE GIFT OF THE MOVIE."

The Battle of Honey Hill was a Civil War battle that occurred in South Carolina on November 30, 1864, during Sherman's "scorched earth" march through the South. That battle, and a modern-day reenactment on the old battlefield, was planned as an epic sequence. The challenge for the production designer was that Louisiana isn't noted for hills. Undaunted, Richard Sherman was out on a scout north of New Orleans, around Saint Francisville, searching for a place to stage the Civil War battle and its reenactment. "I was driving with a location guy when I said, 'Sam! Stop the car!' It was this incredible hill with a lone tree, and there was this valley below. I said, 'This is it.' Four days later, I had Richard LaGravenese in the car, and [I took him there]. He stops the car and looks over and asks, 'Is that it?' I say, 'That's it.' And he starts screaming, 'I can't believe you guys found this!' It really was spectacular. It was the perfect place to do it."

"The Saint Francisville location gave us a beautiful green landscape," Troy Sizemore agreed. "On top of the hill, we put up a present-day cannon monument to the Civil War, where the kids go to hang out. Then certain things, like the monument, had to be removed when we go back in time to the actual Civil War battle. You wanted the feeling that you had gone back in time to the same place."

The Civil War battle was choreographed and planned a month ahead of filming. The action had to account for computer-generated storm effects, the location of more than forty mortars, the placement of the first hundred extras who would be in the line of fire, the positioning of cameras to film it all, and other creative and logistical concerns. "These things are only as good as the planning that goes into them," said producer Erwin Stoff. "We had to plan very, very carefully with special effects, visual effects, stunts. We did pre-viz [pre-visualization], a simple [low-resolution three-D] animated version of the battle to get a sense of what it was going to look like, and made adjustments to that. The challenge of the movie was also the gift of the movie: how to find a way of bringing together all the different worlds

Rachel Brosnahan as Lena's ancestor Genevieve Duchannes.

of the story, from the Civil War to the Casters to young romance."

The location was also prepared for the placement of the pyrotechnic devices and the choreographed movement of the soldiers. "Matt, our effects man, and [I] showed the director how big the bombs were and how I would tie my stunt people into where the explosions would be," stunt coordinator Chuck Picerni explained. "Richard LaGravenese would tell me what he wanted and then give me the freedom to put things together. They buried the explosives [in steel pots], and each pot was laid in with cork and powder. There were wires going from each particular pot to a board where they would hit a button and trigger the effects. I put [stunt] guys into positions where I thought they would work for camera and the kinds of gags they were doing. The first AD [assistant director], Don Sparks, Matt Kutcher, and [I] discussed and coordinated everything that was going to happen. And then visual effects came in and added their flair to where the hurricane and tornado [were] going to be happening, so we placed our action in and among where all that stuff would be. It was a collaboration."

The effects team spent weeks at the location, burying the explosives and marking each spot with tiny flags. Meanwhile, the other departments were

The Civil War battle scene was filmed over three days.

preparing for battle. The prop department hired a seamstress to re-create the Confederate and Union flags, and also borrowed functioning period cannons from Civil War reenactors. Instead of an actual projectile, the cannons would shoot blanks, but otherwise it was the real deal—load, light fuse, fire.

As part of his research into the period props, Brook Yeaton attended some Civil War reenactments. At Port Hudson, outside Saint Francisville, he had a fortuitous encounter with photographer Bruce Schultz, who was taking pictures with an actual tintype camera from the eighteen hundreds. "One of the harder props had been photographs for a family tree that Ethan's mother was in the middle of [compiling] when she passed," Yeaton recalled. "The photographs explain the lineage for Ethan and the witches. Instead of taking digital photographs and making them look like tintypes, I hired Bruce to do actual tintype pictures. He came down to New Orleans and did a still photo shoot for us with our actors lit, in period hair and makeup. You wouldn't be able to tell right away, but my photographer friends

" They brought all these people in with guns, muskets. Suddenly, this battle ensued. The whole place got filled up with smoke, with huge explosions and cannons firing and the people dying! It was amazing to watch. "

—**Richard Sherman,**
production designer

told me there is a difference. That's why I went through this process. It definitely took it to another level."

Fionagh Cush was prepared with a stock of molds for makeup appliances that could be made to re-create bullet wounds, cuts, scrapes, and other physical trauma. "The molds that I have made were designed by makeup artist Greg Funk. They are a genius way for me to always be prepared for pretty much anything, especially on location. I used them on the Civil War, along with a lot of gel blood and dirt. You literally glue them on. They should hold all day, but anything in heat and humidity you're chasing all day long. No matter how strong the glue is, sweat and heat will eventually break it down. That's the biggest challenge when you're outside."

> "I had the 'wow' factor many times on this film, but the Civil War battle was definitely incredible. Our stunt crew really outdid themselves by doing so much of it practical and real."
>
> —**Molly Smith**, producer

The production had to be scrupulous in not only making the fighting look authentic but being true to the soldiers of the period. "That meant the men with contemporary haircuts needed longer hair," Terry Baliel noted. "We put extensions on some of their necklines to make their hair a little longer. Some had wigs for a scraggly, dirty head of hair with length. They all needed period facial hair, so if they had their own mustache, we'd add sideburns or a beard."

The battle was filmed over three days, with an additional three shooting days to stage the reenactment at the same location. To keep the battlefield pristine, production trucks had to be parked a mile away. The prop department

Emma Thompson and Zoe Deutch in period costumes.

brought thirty-five dummies dressed in full wool gear (with makeup adding blood and dirt) that had to be carried to the set, two at a time, up the hill. The production team had a wrangler on the set who was always on the lookout for wild snakes. "It was all glamour, as they say," Yeaton said with a chuckle. "The battle was pretty labor-intensive. And when they had to do the stunts, we had to bring in rubber weapons so no one would get hurt. It was a lot of running back and forth because it was a huge set with very, very wide, epic-style shots. I believe there were fifty guns firing at one time, along with six cannons."

"It was a trip, coming off a massive Civil War picture [*Abraham Lincoln: Vampire Hunter*] right into this one," Matt Kutcher said. "But I have to say that some of the battle sequences in this movie were bigger than what we did for the actual Civil War movie! I'm really proud of what we did. There

Genevieve (Rachel Brosnahan) loses her own Ethan on the battlefield.

Genevieve (Rachel Brosnahan) walks right onto the battlefield to find her love, with explosions going off around her.

were between two [hundred] and three hundred people out on that field, and between the cannons and the guns firing, we had some massive explosions."

"For the sequence, I had about thirty-five stunt people out there," Picerni said. "We had some of the actual Civil War reenactment guys as extras on the battlefield."

Actress Rachel Brosnahan, as Genevieve Duchannes, was integrated into the explosion effects, what Kutcher called "the close-proximity stuff," as she moved through the battlefield.

Costume, hair, and makeup all worked together to present Genevieve and her tragic character arc. "It's not always about making people look pretty," Baliel observed. "You're creating a character. Genevieve is a Caster who goes mad when her lover dies. The actress had very soft, fine hair, so we started with hairpieces for a period look. Then, when she goes mad, her dress and everything about her becomes deteriorated, so we added long, crimped extensions to make her hair almost waist-length and wild and windblown. It was about making the audience understand this person is deranged."

"At one point, she had this beautiful dress and hairstyle, but when she's

on the battlefield and starts the curse, her wardrobe just gets distressed," Cush explained. "Jeffrey decided she should look 'rotting.' ... We added a lot of dirt, sweat, and ash from the gunfire she is walking through. For her makeup, I used Paint Pots by MAC; you're able to smudge them, and [the makeup] held up great in the humidity. The dress was rotting with green, and I took the color from the dress and put it on her face, like splashed paint that's dripping. On the battlefield she looks like a wild woman."

As the actors and extras moved through their exacting and predetermined choreography—"the dance of Civil War people," as Kutcher put it—the explosive elements around them were triggered. "Three of my technicians were firing off these massive boards for the close proximity, based on cues," Kutcher explained. "Most foreground cues came from the actor—they hit their mark, *this* one goes; that stuntman hits this area,

Stuntmen get pulled into the air to react to an explosion during a battle scene.

this one goes. There were a lot of cues. And we had a massive [number] of smoke machines running constantly in the background. We needed very little smoke in the foreground because the explosions going off in the foreground were enough. And we had these big, massive background explosions, each with their own fire station. I had cement powder laid on steel plates with primer cord in between blowing up—we have video of it going up over a hundred feet in the air, and we did multiples of five, six, ten explosions at a time."

There were also supernatural flourishes as Genevieve unleashed her power against the Union soldiers. "She's walking across the battlefield and they say, 'Fire upon her!'" Picerni explained. "When they fire, she reverses the guns on them, so instead of coming out the front, the gun blast is out the back and blows the back of their heads out. For that, we had our stuntmen with blood packs that effects put on [their] front and back, and they all fell down. For another sequence... I had seven guys on a wire, and as explosions went off in front of them, they simultaneously got jerked out on a wire, got blown backward."

During Genevieve's rampage—which an awestruck Ethan and Lena experience in the movie theater—the mad, cursed woman seems to speak directly to Lena about the "cursed women of the Duchannes" family who have

Director Richard LaGravenese with several "soldiers" on set.

Emma Thompson enjoys a moment on set.

been "Claimed to Darkness," as the LaGravenese script describes it. And then Lena has a vision of the women through the generations. "All the women, if they had light eyes, I had to have brown lenses made for them because they're going to have fire in their eyes as a digital effect," Cush explained.

The reenactment was designed as a clear contrast to the Civil War battle. "The reenactment was people dressing up for a Civil War event," Baliel said. "We didn't make that look as perfectly historically correct, so you could tell the difference from the real-life Civil War battle."

Fionagh Cush, admitting that makeup artists sometimes "get overzealous," set up a makeup station in the extras tent to allow reenactors to do their own makeup. "I didn't want it to look like makeup artists had done it. We had done the real Civil War battle the day before, and I wanted it to look like they had done it themselves. We had real reenactors, and they knew what they were doing. They didn't want to look clean, so they put dirt on their hands and face. The big part for us was making sure they were protected from the sun and bugs."

"The reenactors really live for this—they are very hard-core," Richard

THE REENACTMENT FORMS THE BACKDROP FOR THE FULFILLMENT OF LENA'S DESTINY—FOR IT IS THE DATE OF HER FATEFUL SIXTEENTH BIRTHDAY.

Sherman marveled. "And there are also these 'sutlers,' who are all in period clothes and travel around with reenactors. They set up camp with these little trinket shops so that when the public shows up to see the reenactment, they can buy Confederate flags and hats and things. We had to create that, too, and for Matthew Ferguson, the set decorator, that was an interesting job."

Some production principals who had witnessed actual reenactments admired the dedication of the participants but found it a curious phenomenon. "It was interesting to see these wonderful reenactors who were so dedicated to reliving such a tragic and traumatic experience in their history," LaGravenese said. "But it was also an odd experience. Why would they want to reenact a war they lost? That thought had never hit me before. But the idea for the film is they are playacting violence. The Casters are saying, 'Well, here's *real* violence!' And in a way, doesn't one lead to another? Doesn't playacting violence lead to a mentality of war?"

The reenactment forms the backdrop for the fulfillment of Lena's destiny—for it is the date of her fateful sixteenth birthday. Lena appears and crosses the faux battlefield with the same intensity as Genevieve, and conjures a supercell thunderstorm of supernatural proportions. "People have seen tornadoes and thunderstorms, but the idea here is to make them look so beautiful and awe-inspiring that people react to that first—and then it quickly turns violent," visual effects supervisor Harkins explained. "At the end, Lena…creates this giant storm at Honey Hill, where they're having this old Civil War reenactment. It's this boring battle, and almost comedic, but it quickly turns interesting as she brings on this massive storm. When it first appears, Richard wanted it to be awe-inspiring—he referred to the spaceship that appears in *Close Encounters of the Third Kind*. But this storm will be more supernatural, with more lightning, and lightning striking people, even being aggressive, as if it's clearly after mortals and not just an ordinary storm."

When Lena stirs up her megastorm, the tornado sucks up some of the battlefield tents. "That was *not* CG," Kutcher noted. "We had the tents on a spectra line and had a crane with a six-hundred-pound weight. Electronically, by remote control, we dropped the weight. It was two to one, so every foot the weight fell, the tents moved two feet—we dropped the weight sixty feet, and the tents went *zing*ing up into the air. And we did that over and over."

The special effects department provided wind for the Civil War battle and reenactment. "The wind machine is basically the size of a Volkswagen Bug and can go from zero to a premeasured seventy-miles-per-hour wind. Get four of those running on set, that's quite a lot of wind on demand," Kutcher explained.

"When we had to do rain for other scenes, we rented frac tanks that are used in fracture mining and can hold about twenty-four thousand gallons of water each. We sometimes had three or four of them. The water would get pumped up the arm of a crane that held our Spectrum Effects rain bars. It was about one hundred feet in the air, and when you turned the valve on, it made it rain for about the area of a football field."

The reenactment was also the scene for a face-off between Lena and the Dark Caster Sarafine, who finally appears out of the mortal form of Mrs. Lincoln. "She looks like an ominous figure [who] lives in the shadows and enjoys darkness," Joe Harkins said.

During the shooting of the storm sequence, the skies opened up and rain poured down, with howling winds. The freak storm ended filming, although the crew managed to catch some of the elemental fury to use in its storm effects.

"At the Civil War location we saw something like a supercell," recalled Alcon producer Andrew Kosove. "It wasn't a tornado, but it was a cloud the shape of which I had never seen before! It extended down to the ground, was spinning—Broderick and I said, 'Okay! That's the end of the day!'"

Movie
Magic

“*Beautiful Creatures* has really been the most fun imagination ride I've ever had.”

—Richard LaGravenese,
director

Practical special effects were used to create Lena's classroom disruption, and visual effects finished the shots.

Beautiful *Creatures* film editor David Moritz has an envelope stuffed with thirty-five-millimeter VistaVision film frames, pieces of dreams he's held on to since 1990. They are the frames of the matte painting shots from Warren Beatty's *Dick Tracy*, a Disney film that integrated live actors and sets into dramatic glass-painted environments to emulate the comic-strip world of the famed cop with the gun and the two-way wrist radio. It wasn't a virtual world back then, but a photochemical one, and it took imagination, ingenuity, and Machine Age tools to make a director's vision come alive.

"These still frames have been in this envelope for over twenty years, but someday I'm going to make a [reproduction] and put them on my office wall," said Moritz, who had been a visual effects assistant on that production. "*Dick Tracy* was the last movie made in Hollywood that employed matte painting as the art that it was, these oil-painted scenes done on huge glass canvases. There was one shot with a subway miniature and train that passed through a large glass matte painting, just to give a little movement to it. Or you'd shoot Warren and the little boy in the story, and in the [final composite] they would appear as little figures on a big, painted street. Nowadays, you just digitally create or add what you want."

That technological leap from painting on glass to working in the digital realm was underlined during postproduction on *Beautiful Creatures* when an interactive digital tool known as Flame was brought into the editorial suites, along with Flame artist Ryan Yoshimoto, to help design the visual effects sequences Joe Harkins was working on. "Some of the ideas Richard described to me were things I thought Flame could do," Harkins said. "The studio has been very generous to us. A Flame artist usually does commercials or music videos, and occasionally they'll work on films, but it's more of a design-y, interactive job they do with a client and an ad agency.

The hardware alone is expensive, just to rent it. But it was exactly what Richard needed to get the vision he [wanted] on the screen quickly."

Flame artist Yoshimoto was an invaluable resource for figuring out what Harkins called "the Greenbrier flashbacks," with its notion of the past suddenly bleeding through present time. "Visually developing the idea is challenging on still frames," Harkins explained. "We needed animated sequences, and in order to do that, you need something like the Flame. The director can ask for this or that, and the Flame artist can bring it out thirty minutes later. Ryan's background is in design work, and his speed on the Flame gave Richard the interactive feedback he needed to create a multilayered look that no one has seen before. In the long run we're saving time, as well as money, by getting Richard's vision out quicker and with more iterations, more ideas, more collaboration."

LaGravenese's inspiration for the flashbacks included the surreal photography of Scott Mutter, whose 1992 book, *Surrational Images*, featured such strange photomontages as a man wading into a sea with a gigantic escalator looming above him. "I love to juxtapose things, so that was my inspiration for how the flashback comes back. It had to feel like time revealing itself to the present. It's sort of superimposed, so you'd see subtle remnants of the movie theater, like a sconce or EXIT sign up in the trees or [at] the plantation. It was wonderful to play with that with our Flame artist."

On August 2, during postproduction, they cracked the look of the Greenbrier flashback scene. "Richard was like, 'That's *it*, that's really cool, now let's take it to *this* point,'" Moritz said. "We were trying to make it look unique and interesting and very clear that this alternate reality has encircled them and is happening in the movie theater while everyone else is just watching the movie. I'm kind of blown away by the Flame. I'm not so well versed in this amazing technology. But you think of glass paintings on *Dick Tracy* to where we are now, with *Avatar* and the Flame, for heaven's sake. It's the [number] of effects one can create in the Flame, in terms of manipulating the image and adding elements. It's a wonderful machine for the director to get immediate feedback, rather than wait a week to look at some conceptual artwork. It was wonderful for the initial process to get things rolling for shots that were then sent to the big effects houses."

It was a new experience for LaGravenese, having to make the visual effects shots the initial focus of postproduction so that his visual effects supervisor could get things rolling on an estimated five hundred shots. Outside vendors would contract for specific work, from creating supernatural storms to digitally erasing the stunt coordinator's wires and rigs. There was Pixomondo,

Alice Englert filmed in front of a green screen so that the effects of Lena's magic could be added later as special effects.

“I know the story of visual effects, but I can't rattle off the subtle uses of visual effects from the twenties and thirties, like Richard LaGravenese can, even for movies I might have seen but not thought twice about. That was the interesting part for me. You think you know your craft, but somebody comes along and they show you something new that you missed.”

—Joe Harkins,
visual effects supervisor

which had been the lead vendor on *Hugo*. Method Studios, which worked on *Abraham Lincoln: Vampire Hunter* and *Men in Black 3*, would do everything from creating a tornado to inserting magical elements in the family dinner at Ravenwood (along with helping Lena blow Ridley out of the room).

It was also a new experience for Harkins, who had realized his dream of being “on the production side.” His invaluable assistants included concept artist Chuck Boston and “right-hand man” and digital effects supervisor Scott Metzger, who did all the scanning and data collection during principal photography. Harkins seemed to take pride in being able to show the director the tool kit of visual effects, including innovative technology Metzger unveiled in August 2012 at the annual SIGGRAPH computer-graphics convention. “We were able to do several new shots thanks to this technique Scott pioneered,” Harkins explained. “[During principal photography] we had scanned and photographed every single set and were able to pre-viz new shots for Richard with a virtual camera and shoot new plates, virtually. When Scott showed it to people at SIGGRAPH, everyone was blown away. Rather than have to put a set back up, bring in a camera crew, and light the scene again, we had the ability

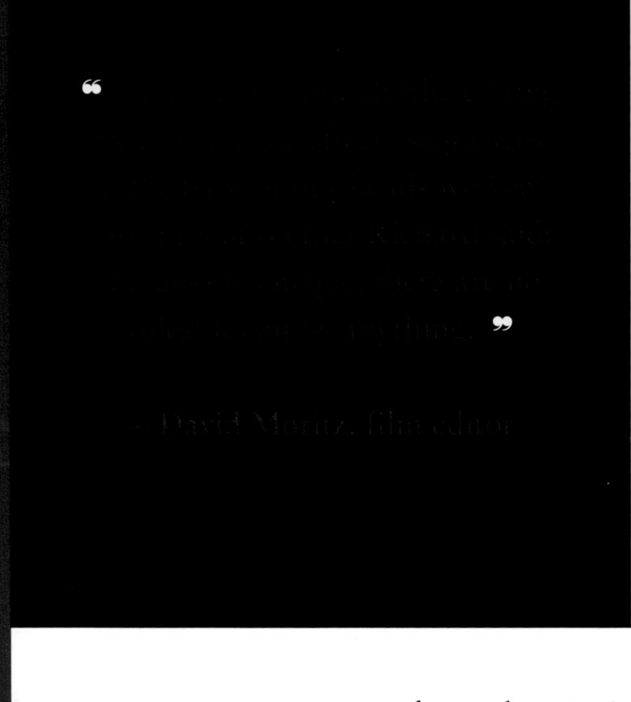

to re-create any scene from the movie with one hundred percent photorealistic accuracy using Scott's techniques."

It was in post that all the work during principal photography came home to roost. Harkins recalled that if a scene had been "event-driven," such as the climactic megastorm, the visual effects work had been planned and executed to precision. "Richard was really comfortable letting us steer that; he trusted us to go on the right path. We'd go over [the effects] with the DP and say, 'Here are the storyboards, here is how we're going to do our day, here are the plates.' And we'd get it."

But when a dialogue scene was combined with visual effects, the director's approach was more fluid, Harkins concluded. "Richard is more actor-centric and open to interpretations of the script. We'd do the normal planning in preproduction, where you plan every day of your shoot and try to stick to that plan. The funny thing with Richard is you'd say, 'It says this in the script.' And he'd say, 'Never mind. I can't believe I wrote that!' And he would immediately brainstorm and figure out something else. The character- and dialogue-oriented stuff could change from minute to minute. You had to be ready to throw up a green screen on the fly, or take it down, or whatever. The script Richard writes versus the script he shoots versus the script that comes to editorial was constantly evolving."

Harkins's insights dovetailed with those of David Moritz, whose mentor (and father-in-law) was Richard Marks, editor for such classics as *Dick Tracy*, *The Godfather: Part II*, and *Apocalypse Now*. "It was his contention, and rightly so, that editing is basically the final rewrite, where the editor and director are in the cutting room together," Moritz said. "There is the movie that one writes, the movie that one shoots, and the movie you edit together and release."

Although the production shot widescreen-format film, the editing process itself would be done digitally. The footage for *Beautiful Creatures* was first processed at a lab in New Orleans and sent to Los Angeles, where it was scanned into an Avid, a digital editing machine. When the work was completed, the digital version could be scanned back out to film for the theatrical release. To keep track of the massive amount of footage, the slates that appeared at the beginning of each shot provided a record of everything from the scene and take number to camera setup and lenses.

"I still think in terms of feet and frames," Moritz admitted. "Some movies may come in at three hundred thousand feet—*Dick Tracy* was almost a million feet, nine hundred thousand feet of film. In the old days you'd just roll it up and look at each take and cut it together with a splicer. You'd have trim bins, like a green metal box, where you'd hang the film on these different pegs. You could have thirty or forty of those bins full after cutting. That was when film was a much more physical endeavor. I don't know if it was better or worse. A picture editor's job is to cut together the movie like in the old days, but now you have eight-tracks of information, where you have dialogue, sound effects, temp music. In the old days, while you were working on the movie, you just had dialogue; music, sound effects, and all that stuff came much later in the process. In our case, we're cutting wide-screen, and

Alice Englert as Lena summons intense emotions, and magic, for the dramatic finale of the film.

there's a lot you can do in an anamorphic frame. It makes cutting different. The close-ups are that much more powerful, the wide shots that much more detail-oriented. There is also a whole lot of visual effects stuff, pieces that won't seem that compelling other than the actors doing a fine job of acting." Those pieces would be completed with the integration of the final approved CG work.

Once the final film was assembled and the negative was ready, it would go through what is called a digital intermediate, or DI, that allowed the director and the director of photography to not only make final color corrections but even manipulate the look of the entire film. "Simply put, if you wanted a scene to feel a little more romantic, you can make a film lean toward a warmer tone," Moritz explained. "If you wanted a scene to feel more isolated and cold, you would lean toward a bluer tone. You're digitally manipulating the image."

Viola Davis observed that both stage acting and movie acting demanded that a performer come from the same place of "truth and honesty." But there was one huge difference between live theater and screen acting, she noted. "Your performance in a movie is in the hands of an editor, so all you have to do on film is sustain a performance for a good twenty to thirty seconds, maybe a minute—that's it! Even if you have a ten-page scene, nobody is going to shoot that in its entirety without cutting. So you can relax in between each part of that ten-page scene. In theater, you have to do the whole scene, and that's one scene in the course of a play. In a play, your character goes on a journey; they're happy and beautiful, and by the

The crew sets up the camera for a tracking shot of the soldiers.

Viola Davis and Alden Ehrenreich on set with director Richard LaGravenese.

end of the play they've killed themselves, they're a puddle of tears and vomit—and you have to figure out how to do that eight times a week. In a movie, you have the vomit expert; you have someone who is going to come in and blow menthol in your eyes to make you look like you've stayed up all night; you have someone with the prop gun, and someone who is going to have the blood."

Talking during the early stages of post, LaGravenese spoke warmly of his entire cast and what he was seeing in the editing room. "The performances are rock solid; the performances are rocking. It's now about how to unfold the elements of the story, because there is so much exposition, and what I need and don't need."

Lena (Alice Englert) offers Ethan (Alden Ehrenreich) a magical moment.

Beautiful Creatures and Beyond

There were many themes in the novel and the movie, such as issues of intolerance and coming-of-age and what it meant to be different, that the filmmakers explored. "What I really liked about the story is that we've all known people whose lives have been affected by the traumas and travails handed down [through] the generations in their own families," producer Erwin Stoff said. "This movie says that no matter what flows down, no matter what is predetermined, I will decide my own fate and my own future. I don't have to accept what has been predetermined."

For Alcon Entertainment's co-CEOs, there is of course a hope that *Beautiful Creatures* will be the start of a franchise. Reflecting during that summer when the film was coming together in the editing suite, Broderick Johnson observed that a franchise, from a business standpoint, provides a bit of a comfort zone in an unpredictable and unforgiving business.

"When you know that you'll have a film every eighteen months over a five-to-six-year period that is going to be profitable, it stabilizes the business in a way that nothing else can," Andrew Kosove concluded. "We've been blessed at Alcon to have some quite successful movies, including the most successful sports film of all time, *The Blind Side.* However, they've all been one-off movies. That said, *Beautiful Creatures* was first things first. This is very much an event film; it is very big and ambitious for a first film. When I look at the film, I go, 'Wow, this was a real undertaking.' We knew we had to make a great movie that would satisfy audiences. We believe we've done that. We'll know soon enough. And if people respond to the story and characters, as we believe they will, then we'll think about sequels. It's too early to think about that right now."

Director Richard LaGravenese sets up a shot with the two lead actors.

Moritz and LaGravenese spent the summer of 2012 together in the editing suite, cutting and honing and adding the effects shots as they came in. Meanwhile, like Lena's countdown tattoo to her Claiming, time relentlessly moved toward their deadline at the end of November.

"There's a mini arc to a scene when the director explains it, and you take the footage and really run with it," Moritz reflected. "You trust your instincts. Where do we want to slow the movie down, where do we want to rock and roll and move forward? Richard, of course, is the prime mover of that. If I can, I offer him [ideas]. You crawl inside a director's head as you sit together for, like, ten weeks. Richard and I did what's called 'stacking,' where every single line reading from every single take and every single camera angle is lined up and we go through it as we assemble the film. If we're in a close-up of Ethan, the director will say, 'Show me all the close-ups for this line reading.' And you go through the close-ups and distill down. But it's an ever-changing and pliable thing. Just because we're picking that selection on the second of August doesn't mean it might not be different on the second of September.

"One time my brother, who's a golf teacher, was sitting on the couch while I was assembling a scene, and he said, 'Is *this* what you do all day long? This is maddening!'" Moritz laughed. "It lost its luster for him very quickly. But as an editor, you're the last one [who] gets the chance to tell the story, to rewrite the movie, and present the movie as it will be cataloged for all time, and that's a really fun thing to do. And when the central aspect is the love affair between two characters, and you see it working, you become invested with them. You're cheering for them. Then it's not about 'How do we make this work?' Then it's a true joy, and all you want to do is make it better. I think that's what we have with Alden and Alice. I never got tired of watching them."

With the final wrap of any production, a cast and crew generally moves on, emotionally as well as physically. But in the afterglow of those long weeks in Louisiana, many in the production reflected on the work.

"The crew were simply wonderful," Emma Thompson summed up. "And as a much older actor than most of the cast, I felt so privileged to be surrounded and playing with some of the best young actors I've ever come across. They all had the vigor and skills of a bunch of veterans. And, of course, we were in the hands of a really terrific director who edited us brilliantly and created a perfect working atmosphere. The strength of the women I was playing, dark though it undoubtedly was, gave me huge pleasure to portray. It's been one of my favorite jobs to date, and I very much hope we all get to do it again."

"Alice used the term 'creating memories,' which I think is true," Alden Ehrenreich said. "From the beginning I felt that we connected on a certain wavelength of ideas and of what we wanted this film to be. When it came time to do the scene, we just kept that dynamic going. And Richard was so open and

Ethan (Alden Ehrenreich) with his best friend, Link (Thomas Mann).

receptive to all of our ideas. He gave us the freedom to experiment and come up with more interesting, or even absurd, choices than you would find if you were just trying to 'get it right' on the first take. I personally like a lot of takes so I can try different things, and he allowed me to do that. He was always dedicated to bringing out the most human angle of the story and [having] that lead the magic and effects, as opposed to the other way around.

Emmy Rossum as Ridley.

"It was also a real honor to work with the 'veteran' actors. In fact, on certain days when I wasn't needed, I would come to set just to watch a scene with Viola and Jeremy, or Emma and Jeremy. I thought of it like acting school, which it was. They were all very open with their ideas and supported Alice and [me] in all our scenes."

Zoey Deutch, making her big-screen debut in *Beautiful Creatures*, recalled that although she wasn't in scenes with Jeremy Irons or Viola Davis, she was

Zoey Deutch poses for a few candid shots.

Alden Ehrenreich makes a friend on set.

in the background for some pivotal Emma Thompson scenes. "I had to keep reminding myself that it was both real and also the greatest master class in acting I've ever had. She is so patient, honest, and hilarious, and instantly makes you feel comfortable, like you belong. There's no doubt I have a lifelong friend crush on her."

Art director Lorin Flemming felt the film had a classic look. "It's like a beautiful old movie. At the end of filming we had a crew party, and they did a slide show of all the different sets, and they were pretty grand."

"I loved the first set that's in the script," production designer Richard Sherman reflected. "The opening up outside of Ethan's bedroom and coming in the window, where we see him lying in bed reading this story before he heads off on his midnight run. The odd thing was that what I imagined in my head, we built—the exact same thing. In Ethan's room we see all this lathe and plaster, like the way old houses were constructed with flats of wood and plaster oozing through it. To go from the very rough, raw interior of Ethan's attic bedroom into the very, very esoteric interior of Ravenwood, which is someone's whim, was amazing."

Fionagh Cush recalled that when she read the first draft of the script, it all seemed so simple. "I didn't think it was going to be a challenging movie at all. But it crossed so many borders, from Civil War period to fantasy to tribal stuff. It had a little bit of everything. And just working with Terry [Baliel], whom I'd never worked with before, was, if anything, the highlight of my career. He was so brilliant, and an inspiration to everybody. And Richard, our director, had such a great vision and was really articulate about what he wanted. And then he just trusted us and allowed us to do our own thing. It worked out brilliantly. It was a good team."

"It was a very collaborative effort for everybody, and Richard set it up that way," Jeffrey Kurland added. "He wanted it that way. He chose everybody very specifically so that we would all be at the top of our game and happy to be doing this together. Hopefully, we were able to present these worlds that exist within the *Beautiful Creatures* scenario, and... we've given it that depth and life that goes beyond the printed page."

They had all conjured up that world—like magic. Movie magic. Georges Méliés, that stage magician and primal wizard of all movie magic to come—the man who created in a studio made of glass as the illusions he captured on camera shone with the sun—knew a thing or two about "giving the appearance of reality to the most chimerical dreams."[6] Even in those seminal early years, it took costume and makeup and hair, sets and props, pyrotechnics and more for Méliés to pull off one of his elaborate "trick" films.

"You always have magic days on a movie, certainly," said Troy Sizemore. "There are definitely magic moments. It's like, 'Wow, look at what we're doing.' Or you're up in the swamp at dawn and the sun is coming through the mist and there are alligators in the water and you

can hear the big bull alligator croaking on the other side."

"To me, it feels like a circus," Brook Yeaton reflected. "We set up our tents, we do our thing, we make magic every day. And every day is different, and every day is an adventure. I tried to walk away from this business when I had my daughter—and got myself right back into it as soon as I could! Now, I'm re-inspired, and I don't take it for granted. Every day on set is a good day. I just love the industry. I love making movies, watching movies, talking movies, breathing movies. It's what I do."

"Yes, when a movie comes together, it is magical," Richard LaGravenese concluded. "And this film, out of [everything I've written] and directed, had more moments when I went, 'Wow! That's exactly how I imagined it.' Or it was even better. And that was because of everybody coming together. And part of the experience is the relationship between an audience's imagination and yours. It's strange that in this interactive world of the Internet, movies now are often the opposite of interactive—they just blast you with stimuli. It's just numbing, and in terms of character and story I'm not feeling anything. To me, it's more interesting to ask the audience to participate in the imagination."

Kosove pondered the marketing

Ethan (Alden Ehrenreich) wears a harness to film the stunt where Lena (Alice Englert) "helps" him climb down from her room.

A happy director with his crew and cast.

campaign that would eventually be fired up. He likened it to a very good pasta sauce that is full of delicious ingredients, but you couldn't overdo any one. Similarly, this new genre had a lot of rich ingredients—young romance, fantasy, mystery and intrigue, dramatic set pieces. But Kosove put his finger on that essential ingredient that had moved the authors when they began writing a fantasy novel on a dare. "Unlike a lot of these other movies, our female protagonist isn't a deer caught in the headlights. Our female protagonist is the strength of the movie. She's the one with the power, with all the special things happening. We feel we have a real female-empowerment movie for women of all ages."

Richard LaGravenese had been similarly attracted to that theme of independence. *This is who I am*. But as he entered the world of *Beautiful Creatures* and became immersed in it, another idea came to him. . . .

"What I discovered while writing the script was that love and power couldn't coexist. It was about the curse and Lena's love and Lena changing the rules because of love. It's interesting to me that Casters have the power to control everything, but they don't understand a lot of things about humanity that are actually very strong powers *we* have.

"I don't know if it'll make it into the movie, but one of the last scenes I wrote before we went into production was a scene between Macon and Ethan. Macon says, 'I never understood your species. You have no real powers; you have no real control over anything. Yet you think that by what you feel, everything will turn out all right.' And Ethan says, 'Well, sometimes you just have to have a little faith.' In that one little moment, you see that Casters haven't developed those powers that we have, and that we have to develop, because of what it means to be human. Things like faith and sacrifice and love. So it became a story about the strength of humanity. That's what I discovered."

> "While we worked, Richard [LaGravenese] was constantly rewriting and adjusting the script to fit what was evolving during the shoot. He made it a very inclusive process and was very open to the actors' ideas as their characters became more concrete. It can sometimes be an advantage to have the writer as director."
>
> —Jeremy Irons, actor

NOTES

1: Kami Garcia & Margaret Stohl, *Beautiful Creatures* (New York and Boston: Little, Brown and Company, 2009), p. 2.

2: Geoffrey C. Ward, with Ric Burns and Ken Burns, *The Civil War: An Illustrated History* (New York: Alfred A. Knopf, Inc., 1990), pp. 332–333.

3: Garcia & Stohl, *Beautiful Creatures*, p. 2.

4: Garcia & Stohl, *Beautiful Creatures*, p. 64.

5: *Grand Palais* Paris website: www.grandpalais.fr/visite/en

6: Georges Méliés, *Cinematographic Views*, 1907, as reprinted: Emmanuelle Toulet, *Birth of the Motion Picture* (New York: Harry N. Abrams, 1995), p. 142.

ACKNOWLEDGMENTS

I'm grateful to Erin Stein at Little, Brown for sending me into the world of *Beautiful Creatures*, and to Jennifer Robertson at Alcon Entertainment, who helped me find my way around when I got there.

I'm especially grateful to the creative people who shared their insights and reflections—you are all Light Casters! And to those who helped facilitate: David Leatherwood, Richard LaGravenese's assistant; Alexander Cooke in the office of Christian Hodell, for connections to Emma Thompson (and Viv Irish, Emma's assistant); Sally Fischer for Jeremy Irons; Jessica Carrera for getting my questions to Alice Englert; Robyn Johnson and Angela Taylor in Erwin Stoff's office; Stephanie Gonzalez, Christine Tripicchio, and the staff at WKT Public Relations, who connected me with Viola Davis; Chris Contopulos at Brillstein Entertainment Partners for Alden Ehrenreich; Gordon Gilbertson for Zoey Deutch; Matthew Rasmussen for setting up time with Andrew Kosove and Broderick Johnson; and to anyone I might have missed.... Thank you all for the courtesy and consideration.

My thanks to my agent, John Silbersack, for his energy, dedication, and diligence, and to his assistant, Rachel Mosner, who always keeps things under control. Love to my dear Edris for her patience and support, and to my mother, Bettylu, who is the last word when it comes to proofreading my manuscripts.

And to Mike Wigner, World's Greatest Bike Messenger: Wig, it's a wrap—see you at Vesuvio's!

AUTHOR'S CREDITS

Mark Cotta Vaz is the author of the #1 *New York Times* bestselling *Twilight Saga* movie companion series. He is the author of more than thirty books, including *Industrial Light + Magic: Into the Digital Realm*, a history of the second decade of George Lucas's famed visual effects house; the award-winning *The Invisible Art: The Legends of Movie Matte Painting* (coauthored with Academy Governor and Oscar winner Craig Barron); and the critically acclaimed *Living Dangerously: The Adventures of Merian C. Cooper, Creator of King Kong*. His recent books include *Batmobile: The Complete History* and *The Host Movie Companion Book*.

Photo by Bruce Walters

Read the beginning of the story in these exclusive editions of *Beautiful Creatures*!

LITTLE, BROWN AND COMPANY
BOOKS FOR YOUNG READERS